Collector's Guide To

MADE in JAPAN

Ceramics

Identification & Values

BOOK II

Carole Bess White

COLLECTOR BOOKS

A Division of Schroeder Publishing Co., Inc.

The current values of this book should be used only as a guide. They are not intended to set prices, which vary from one section of the country to another. Auction prices as well as dealer prices vary greatly and are affected by condition as well as demand. Neither the Author nor the Publisher assumes responsibility for any losses that might be incurred as a result of consulting this guide.

Searching for a Publisher?

We are always looking for knowledgeable people considered to be experts within their fields. If you feel that there is a real need for a book on your collectible subject and have a large comprehensive collection, contact Collector Books.

Photographs by: Les White
Cover Design: Sherry Kraus
Book Design: Donna Ballard

On the cover: Pair of Bird Candlesticks in multicolored matte glazes, 5½", Black Mark #1, pair $100.00 – 150.00. Art Deco bowl with lady in tan and multicolored luster and matte glazes, 8¼" wide, Red Mark #56, $25.00 – 50.00. Rare bellhop liquor set in multicolored shiny glazes, 11", decanter Black Mark #1, shot glasses no Mark, $100.00 – 155.00. Dutch boy perfume in multicolored luster and shiny glazes, 3½" Red Mark #1, $50.00 – 85.00. Vase in tan luster glaze with multicolored floral motif, 5½", Red Mark #1, $30.00 – 50.00.

Additional copies of this book may be ordered from:

Collector Books
P.O. Box 3009
Paducah, Kentucky 42002-3009

@ $18.95. Add $2.00 for postage and handling.

Copyright: Carole Bess White, 1996

Printed by IMAGE GRAPHICS, INC., Paducah, Kentucky

⋇ Contents ⋇

Chapters are in alphabetical order, and pieces are alphabetized within the chapters.

◁ Dedication ▷

This book is respectfully and thankfully dedicated to the workers in the ceramics industries of Japan, whose labor throughout the years give collectors so much pleasure today.

◁ Acknowledgments ▷

Thanks to Mr. Keishi Suzuki, President of Noritake Sales, Ltd., Senior Managing Director of Noritake Co., Limited, President of the Japan Pottery Exporters' Association, for securing most of the new information on Marks and companies, and for introducing us to the helpful folks at the Japan Pottery Exporters' Association. Without his help, there would be precious little new information in this book!

Thanks to Mr. Susumu Kondo, Managing Director of the Japan Pottery Exporters' Association, and Mr. Kiyoshi Kosakai, Deputy Secretary General of the Japan Pottery Design Center, for invaluable information on marks and backstamps.

Thanks to Mr. MaSao Oki, General Secretary of the Japan Pottery Design Center, for letting us look at the books of designs from 1955 to the present.

Thanks to Dr. Kohei Yoshido for invaluable referrals in Japan.

Thanks to Mr. Yashiro Nakano, Curator, and Mr. Toshio Ando, Director, of the Aichi Prefectural Ceramic Museum; and to Mr. Fumitaka Hattori, Curator, Seto-Shi Rekishi Minzoku Shiryokan.

Thanks to Mr. Yutaka Kato, President of the Maruyama Corporation, for sharing his wonderful factory and its history.

Thanks to Mr. Bill Naito of Norcrest China for lending the catalog pages that appear at the end of this book.

Thanks to Susan Farwell, who practically had to hold the backdrop with her teeth as we took impromptu photos in California.

Thanks to Miss Asami Takeuchi, translator, guide, and assistant in Japan.

Thanks to Miss Elizabeth Brewer, photo assistant in Oregon.

Thanks to collectors and dealers everywhere who shared their knowledge, and their collections. Without them this book would not have been possible:

Mary Ann and Bob Sloan of Main Street Antique Mall in Toledo, Oregon, not only brought their entire Made in Japan collection to Portland, they also brought all their additional pieces to be photographed as they acquired them.

Colleen Bulger and Dan Torres of Antique Alley in Portland, Oregon, let us come to their store several times to photograph their extensive stock of Made in Japan.

Nirmal Kaur Khalsa, Sewa Singh and Sewa Kaur Khalsa, Pat and Harold Moyer, and Trudi and Frank Peters let us come to their homes and photograph their entire collections of wonderful and interesting Made in Japan.

Members of Portland's Rain of Glass Club, as well as many other collectors and dealers, contributed pieces: Their generosity resulted in more pictures than this book would hold!

Janice Ahl	Jewell Gowan	Floyd Pearson and Skip Schaeffer
Lucille Babcock	Mable Hardebeck	Cracker Barrel Antiques,
Betty Bain	Lillian Hodges	Lakehead, CA
Shirley Bolman	Angie Haynes	Frank and Trudi Peters
Lizzie, John, Bill, and Nancy Brewer	Gyrid Hyde-Towle	Cathy Pisaneschi
Colleen Bulger and Ron Torres	Nirmal Kaur Khalsa	Debbie Phillips
Lea and Ron Burcham	Sewa Singh and Sewa Kaur Khalsa	Don and Helen Proctor
Candy Bussell	Grace and Jim Livingston	Agnes Rytkonen
Dave Coons	Main Street Antique Mall,	David and Jannie Spain
Carrie and Gerry Domitz	Los Gatos, CA	Mary Ann and Bob Sloan
Donna Edgar	Sandy Millius	W. Joanne Voeller
Jan Edmonson	Fern Moist	Jan and Ernie Weaver
Susan Farwell	Pat and Harold Moyer	Joe Webb of Antique Promenade,
Jeff Gassner	Tomoko Nakashima	Sacramento, CA
		Jim Vanek

Write if you collect Made in Japan, would like to share information or subscribe to the Made in Japan Info Letter, or order autographed copies of this book. Please enclose a self-addressed stamped envelope.

Carole Bess White
P.O. Box 819
Portland, OR 97207
FAX (503) 281-2817

⚞ The Data ⚟

⚞ Carole's Excellent Adventure, or How I Spent My Summer Vacation ⚟

Besides "What is it worth?" the two questions collectors most often ask are: "How old is it?" and "Who Made it?" It seemed to me that they could best be answered in Japan, so there I went in the summer of 1995. I went by myself, but I had a great translator, Asami Takeuchi, to help me because I speak virtually no Japanese. Did I find all the answers? No. But I got a very good start, and this book contains the new facts I learned.

The ceramics business in Japan is a shrinking industry. There are still large companies such as Noritake and Mikasa producing lovely ceramics in great quantities for worldwide consumption, but the smaller producers have largely disappeared. It is sad to see the demise of a once-great industry.

Nagoya, Japan, was established as an international port in 1907. For the next 45 years, including the years that Japan was fighting World War II, pottery was the largest category of exports shipped from Nagoya. Today, that has shrunk to about 1%, and cars and machines have become the largest export. What does this mean to collectors?

As for older collectibles, not much — because Japan exported literally millions of ceramics over the years. This means that there is a substantial supply of pieces here in America for us to collect, if we can only find them!

As for newer collectibles, it's anybody's guess. However, keep in mind that everything new becomes old at some time in the future.

As for research, there's the challenge. With so many companies closed, employees scattered or deceased, and records lost, it is difficult to track down much of what went on before 1955. The Japan Pottery Design Center has record books with pictures of every single design that was made in Japan from 1955 on, and this is a valuable resource not only because of what's in the books, but because of what's not in them. It would take a very long sabbatical to adequately study these hundreds of thousands of pictures; I had only a day. But I did get a wonderful sense of confirmation of what's "new" (by which I mean post-1955.) However, the pictures are almost all in black and white, so it was impossible to tell what types of glazes were used.

In the same building is the Japan Pottery Exporters' Association, and there, thanks to Mr. Keishi Suzuki, President of Noritake Sales, Ltd., Senior Managing Director of the Noritake Co., Ltd., and President of the association, I was allowed to study some of the thousands of pages of marks that were used by Japanese ceramics companies. They were able to tell me when many of the companies opened and closed, and this information might be as close as we'll ever get to dating pieces. (See the "New Information on Companies" chart for this information.) In my own mind I feel sure that, with the exception of the indisputable marks that are dated, such as Mark 7, or the ones on obvious post-war pieces, many of the "unknown" marks in this book are probably pre-World War II because if they were from after the war, they would be known to the association.

Still the questions remain:
Can Japanese Ceramics be dated by ink color of the backstamp?

Can Japanese Ceramics be dated by whether they are marked Japan or Made in Japan?

According to every single one of the lifetime ceramics industry experts in Japan whom I was fortunate to discuss this with, the answer to both questions is no!!

There are several different combinations of the above theories that many American collectors still would like to believe are accurate ways to date pieces. Collectors like absolutes when it comes to dating, but there is no easy way to tell if your pieces are pre- or post-World War II by backstamp colors or wording. Why? Because Japanese ceramics during and just after the Occupation were made either from pre-war molds, or they were made in the same style as successful pre-war pieces. This makes it virtually impossible to say whether older-looking pieces are from before the war or from the years immediately following it!

Technology and techniques improved rapidly after the war, and ceramic styles had changed radically by 1955, so it is fairly simple to tell if pieces are pre- or post-1955.

According to Mr. Kiyoshi Kosakai of the Japan Pottery Design Center, most of the pieces in *The Collector's Guide to Made in Japan Ceramics, Volume I*, are pre-1955, and, of these, most are probably pre-war.

Except for the obviously newer pieces, most pieces in this book, *The Collector's Guide to Made in Japan Ceramics, Volume II*, are also pre-1955, and, again, of these, most are probably pre-war.

⊰ Chronicle of Made in Japan Ceramics ⊱

The United States Customs Bureau enforces the law on marking imported goods. This law determined how Japanese ceramics were back stamped through the years. As American laws changed, the backstamps were changed to conform.

1891 – 1921	**NIPPON/HAND PAINTED NIPPON** Before 1891, goods exported to America did not have to be stamped with their country of origin in English. Japanese ceramics usually had no backstamps, or they had artists' or their patrons' names in Japanese characters. The McKinley Tariff, which took effect March 1, 1891, required that all imported goods had to be stamped in English with their country of origin. At the time, "Nippon" was considered to be an acceptable name for Japan, so most Japanese ceramics of this period were backstamped "Nippon" or "Hand Painted Nippon," often with a company logo as well. However, not all were stamped that way. There were still unmarked pieces, and pieces stamped "Japan" as well. Nippon pieces are priced higher than most Made in Japan and are eagerly sought by collectors.
1921 – 1941	**NORITAKE ART DECO** The Noritake Art Deco pieces are considered the "Cadillac" of Made in Japan ceramics by many collectors. They were consistently the best quality and most beautifully decorated, and today they are very avidly collected and are priced accordingly.
1921 – 1941	**EARLY MADE IN JAPAN** The U.S. Customs Bureau ruled that "Nippon" was no longer an acceptable synonym. As of August 1, 1921, all goods were supposed to be backstamped "Japan." Technically, the MIJ era began when the Nippon era ended in 1921, but it really was not that precise. At some point the U.S. Customs Bureau may have required that the words "Made In" be added to the backstamps, but this was not always done. Unmarked pieces sometimes slipped through Customs, but most of the ceramics from 1921 to 1941 are marked either "Japan" or "Made in Japan." Sometimes, all pieces in a set are not backstamped. The profit margin on ceramics was slim, and a factory could save a little labor cost by not marking every piece in a set. If pieces in a set have different backstamps, it is because there often was not room for "Made in Japan," or a company logo, so they just used "Japan" on some of the smaller pieces. Early Made in Japan pieces, especially Art Deco and lusters, have come into their own and are very collectible.
1947 – 1952	**OCCUPIED JAPAN/MADE IN OCCUPIED JAPAN** When America and Japan went to war in 1941, trade ceased, so no new shipments of Made in Japan were imported. However, pieces already in this country continued to sell. After the war, the United States occupied Japan from September 2, 1945, until April 28, 1952. The Occupied Japan backstamp era truly began August 15, 1947, when ceramics companies again were allowed to engage in private foreign trade. The U.S. Customs Bureau decreed in 1949 that Japanese goods could be marked "Occupied Japan," "Made in Occupied Japan," "Japan," or "Made in Japan." Again, some were not marked at all. Occupied ware has its ardent collectors as well, but prices seem to be about equal to or (in some cases) lower than early Made in Japan.
1952 – Today	**POST-WAR MADE IN JAPAN** When the Occupation ended in 1952, marks no longer contained the word "Occupied," so pieces were again marked only with "Japan" or "Made in Japan." This is when the paper label era really began. Prior to WW II, paper labels were flimsy and the glue was often not strong, so the Customs Bureau usually made importers replace the labels with indelible ink backstamps. In the fifties, technology improved and paper labels were allowed. The two most common types of labels seem to be: •Small oval or rectangular blue or black paper with white letters •Two-color metallic, such as black or red with gold or silver lettering. The real sleepers are the post-WW II Made in Japan pieces because they are still very affordable!

The area around Nagoya, including Aichi, Gifu, and Mie Prefectures, has always been Japan's largest production center of export commercial ceramics. This area has a very large supply of good clay and fuel. But more importantly, early Nagoya area producers quickly began changing from traditional pottery styles to commercial ceramics when Japan expanded its foreign trade in the 19th century, while those in other areas did not. The map shows the section of Nagoya around the original Noritake factory as of June 1934. Just in that fairly small area were family/cottage and secondary ceramics industries (▲), decoration factories (●), exporters (O), decorator-exporters (◉), whiteware manufacturers (☆), and industrial association offices(◐).

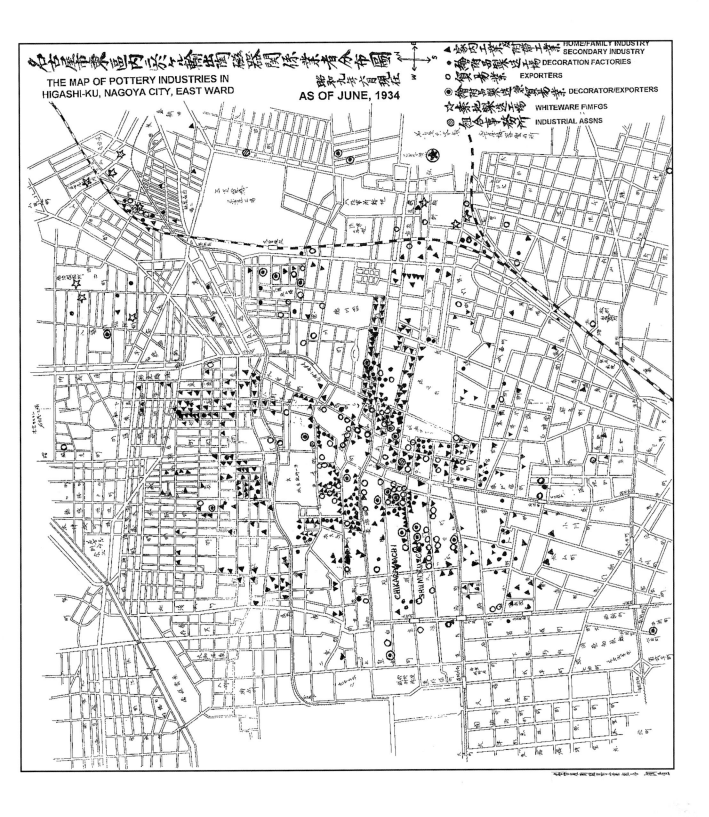

During the Nippon era, Japan began manufacturing and exporting their first novelties: Western style toys and dolls. In the beginning, the Japanese producers copied German originals. The first ones were simple Indian dolls, small bisque figurines made for export to India. Next came bisque dolls for export to the United States. These were made in plaster molds. As time went on, the molds became more elaborate, and many Japanese ceramics equaled or surpassed Germany's in quality and workmanship.

Because of World War I, the Germans were unable to continue exporting novelties to America, and Japan stepped in to fill the gap this created. In addition to dolls, they made toys, incense burners, and flower vases. As their skill increased, so did the number and types of items they manufactured.

The American stock market crashed on October 29, 1929. As economic conditions worsened during the Great Depression, the desire for cheap, colorful, and attractive novelties and dishes grew. Made in Japan ceramics filled that need.

(This, along with the advent of American-made Depression glass, had a profound effect on the American ceramics industry. By 1934, Japan's share of the total quantity of dinnerware imported by America had risen from 51% to 85%. Figures from 1935 show that Japan shipped 36.9% of their total ceramic exports to the United States. To counter the competition, American manufacturers produced colorful pottery dinnerware, such as Fiesta, but that's another story! Note that the Japanese dinnerware was designed for home use, so it is thin and translucent. Before 1935, Japan had also exported hotel dinnerware to the United States, but they had to decrease this to avoid conflict with our ceramic companies.)

Throughout the 1920s and 1930s, Japanese producers expanded their novelty lines, incorporating household articles and smoking sets; ashtrays both with and without animal or human figures; table and kitchen ware such as salt and pepper shakers; honey, jam, and pickle containers; cheese plates; egg cups; napkin holders, toothpick holders; plaques and wall plates; bathroom accessories such as cups, soap dishes, and toothbrush holders; bookends; ink stands; pin trays; photo frames; candlesticks and lamps; planters; coin and razor banks; liquor items; cosmetic articles such as perfume bottles and powder boxes; and much more. (The Japanese manufacturers refer to nearly everything that is not tableware, or sets of china dishes, as novelties.)

German original calendar, 4¾", marked "Germany 18388," $25.00 – 55.00.

Also, technology improved and they were able to produce high quality figurine dolls with baroque or rococo style costumes of the 17th and 18th centuries. (American collectors often call these figurines colonials.) By 1937, novelties were 11.4% of Japan's total ceramic exports. The United States received the lion's share of these: 69.3%. By 1939, the United States had dropped back to second place, behind China, in receiving ceramic exports from Japan. During World War II, Japan did not produce novelties because they could not get raw materials. They did continue to produce tableware, but not for export to America.

During the first years of the Occupation, the Japanese tried to imitate or recreate the same types of novelties that did so well for them before World War II. As time went on, production techniques improved. An example: lace dolls, the figurines with the real lace applied to the skirts. Before WWII, the Japanese manufacturers were just able to produce plain figurines. after, they had the technology to apply the lace ruffles to them. As the fifties progressed, the old styles were dropped from manufacturers' lines, and new styles replaced them.

Japan has exported more than 750,000 tableware patterns to the United States, and probably close to that number of novelties. (Keep in mind that we are talking about patterns, not blanks, on the dishes. This means that several different patterns could have been applied to the same china blanks, or shapes.)

German "original" cigarette set in tan luster, 8" wide, marked 'IMPORTE D' ALLEMAGNE' (French for "made in Germany"), $25.00 – 55.00.

✍ New Information on Companies ✍

Most of the Japanese ceramics companies have closed entirely or moved to other countries where labor is cheaper. This means that many records that miraculously survived the war are now lost or destroyed, and workers have scattered. I was able to obtain new information from Mr. Suzuki and the Japan Pottery Exporters' Association, and I will continue my research and hope to add more as time goes by. *Toki* is Japanese for chinaware or pottery; *Kaisha* means company; *Boeki* means international trade; *Shokai* means trading company (used mainly for wholesale businesses); and *Shoten* means store or trading house, and is used either for retail or wholesale businesses.

MARKS 1 – 4, 40 No specific company. Nearly all companies used variations of these marks at one time or another	MARK 58 Nagoya Boeki Shokai, still in business
MARKS 5-9, 13-19, 22, 23A, 27, 29, 33-39, 41, 46, 50-52, 55-56, 62, 66-67, 72-74, 76-98, 100-103, 105-110, 112 unknown	MARK 59 Nanri Boeki & Co., closed 1978
MARK 10 Shofu Industrial Co., LTD., in business before WWII, closed September of 1965	MARKS 60-61 Mogi Shoji & Co., still in business
MARKS 11, 12, 12A, 21, 21A, 32, 43, 43A, 44 Tashiro Shoten LTD., in business before WWII, closed 1954	MARK 63 Yokoi Sei-ichi Shoten, closed 1942
MARKS 20, 24, 25, 30, 30A Seyei Toki Co., Ltd., Nagoya. In business before World War II, discontinued exporting their products in the 1970s. (Mark 30A was registered in 1932.)	MARK 64 Nagoya Seito Sho, in business before WWII, closed 1969
MARK 23 Nihon Yoko Boeki Co., still in business	MARK 65 Yamashiro Ryuhei (later changed to Maruyama Toki), opened in 1914, stopped production 1989
MARKS 26, 53, 54 Nippon Toki Kasha (Noritake Co., limited) founded 1876, still in business	MARK 68 Iwata (could be name of manufacturer or exporter) closing date unknown
MARK 28 Hotta Yu Shoten & Co., in business before WWII, closed 1947	MARKS 69 & 70 Manufactured in Japan for the American Company, Joséf originals, from 1955 through the early 1970s
MARK 31 Maruka Tajimi Boeki Shokai, still in business	MARK 71 Aichi Toki Shokai (formerly Higo Hoten), still in business
MARK 42 Enesco, Japan, closed in November 1978	MARK 75 Narumi China Corporation, Nagoya, registered this Mark in 1934. (Refer to Melto China Information following this chart.)
MARK 45 Hanai Giryo Co., in business before WWII, closing date unknown	MARK 99 Shimizu-rokunosuko Shoten, Nagoya, registered this Mark in 1932. They closed before World War II.
MARKS 47 & 48 Tsujisoo Toki Co. In Book I Mark #44 was substituted for MARK #48. MARK #48 is correct in this book.	MARK 104 Marugo Seito sho Inc., Tokoname City, Aichi Prefecture, registered this Mark in 1950. They stopped production in the 1980s.
MARK 49 Kinkozan, 1645 – 1927	MARK 111 Empire Trading Co., Ltd., Nagoya, which had no factory, registered this Mark in 1950. They closed their business in the 1980s.
MARK 57 United China & Gift Co. (formerly United China & Glass Co.), still in business	

Goldcastle (Marks 43, 43a, 44)

The company that used these marks, Tashiro Shoten Ltd., of Nagoya, closed in 1954. CHIKUSA, which appears on Marks 43 and 43a, is the name of a district in the Nagoya area. Tashiro Shoten also sold pieces with Marks 11, 12, 12a, 21, 21a, and 32.

Kinkozan, Mark 49

A family of potters named Kagiya began producing wares in Kyoto in 1645. In 1756 their name was changed to Kinkozan when the patriarch was named "official potter" to the Shogunate of Tokugawa. Kinkozan is best known for Satsuma ware, but they produced other types of commercial ware as well, including art pottery and wonderful Art Deco pieces. After nearly 300 years in production, Kinkozan ended in 1927. Thus, pieces bearing this mark are not only pre-World War II but are very early examples of Made in Japan, because the marking laws changed in 1921.

Noritake Co., LTD. (Marks 26, 53, 54)

Mark #26, the cherry blossom, has been officially identified as Noritake by Mr. Keishi Suzuki, President of Noritake Sales Ltd. This mark was used on second grade whiteware (unglazed pieces). What great news for collectors, who have long suspected it to be true.

Mr. Suzuki also confirmed that the green oak leaf Noritake marks designated first grade whiteware, and blue designated second grade. For the Noritake backstamps *only*, different ink colors might also signify different decoration factories (subsidiary decorators). However, it is not known today which ink colors represented which factories, if any. Noritake used five different ink colors on backstamps, but their meaning has been lost.

Noritake had their own whiteware factory, but they also purchased whiteware from companies in Seto. They had exclusive contracts with about five different suppliers.

For a Made in Japan collector, the Noritake factory in Nagoya, Japan, is an experience not to be missed. There is a very interesting model factory, with workers demonstrating all facets of ceramics production. The star of the show is a fabulous museum with pieces from throughout Noritake's history. There you will see items from the Nippon era, the Noritake Art Deco Era, and modern pieces as well. There is also a "Gallery of Tabletop," with displays of modern Noritake dinnerware in table settings with wonderful accessories. There is a shop at the factory, but there is an even bigger retail outlet in downtown Nagoya. (Both stores sell only current pieces, although there is a line of reproduction items as well. These are clearly marked, so it is easy to tell them from the antique originals.) If you are a Noritake fan, you should try to get there. (Please call ahead for a visit.) There are also factories in the Kyushu area, as well as the Philippines, Sri Lanka, and Ireland.

Meito China/Nagoya Seito Sho (Mark 64)

Mr. Kotero Asukai, a founder and one of the engineers of the Noritake Company, "retired" from Noritake about 1908. He took about 30 workers with him, and he opened the Nagoya Seito Sho Company and produced Meito China. This is why early Meito China looks so much like Noritake ware! During World War II, Sumitomo Steel Industry Company purchased the company and changed the name to Narumi Seito Sho. Narumi is still in business producing bone china, which they supply to Mikasa.

Maruyama Toki (originally called Yamashiro Ryuhei) (Mark 65)

This company no longer manufactures ceramics, but Mr. Yutaka Kato still owns the premises and was willing to share his history — and what a history it is!

The factory is up and over hills in what now looks to be a residential area of Seto, Japan. To enter it is to step back in time. The main building looks like it was built in the 1920s, but the outbuildings look a bit older than that. Just inside the door of the main building, there is a step up into a tiny formal meeting room furnished with a classic pink plush sofa and chairs. The rest of the offices look like they came out of a romantic old black and white movie.

Upstairs is a room of wonder—a two-part showroom of samples of older novelties, some of which I had never seen before, as well as pieces from their more recent history including a series of lady figurines for Lennox, and Norman Rockwell figural groupings for the Franklin Mint. I thought I had died and gone to Made in Japan Heaven, or perhaps I had been reincarnated as Howard Carter opening King Tut's tomb. But there was more!

A catwalk of planks led across to the warehouse, in which are stored boxes with a sample of every piece made year by year since 1914. What a treasure trove! Time was short, but I was able to look into several of the boxes. It was amazing to see the history of Made in Japan novelties right before my eyes, box by box, year by year.

The Maruyama Corporation began making novelties in 1914. Their first pieces were Indian dolls, which were shipped to "the south," which to Japan is India. Later they were exported to Thailand, the United States, and European countries as well. They expanded their line to include ceramic carp to decorate ponds and fishbowl ornaments. Maruyama was the Japanese source for all the early novelties. According to Mr. Kato, they "borrowed" from the German designs, then the other Japanese manufacturers copied Maruyama, especially after World War I.

Maruyama produced every conceivable sort of novelty through the years. The pieces are attractive and very appealing. Collectors today find Mark #65 most often on figurines ("dolls"), pincushions, and planters. However, like most Japanese manufacturers, Maruyama marked their pieces three different ways: with Mark #65, with "Made in Japan," or with "Japan." Maruyama remained a leading manufacturer of ceramics in Japan until they ceased production in 1989.

⚐ Japanese Periods ⚐

Collectors of fine Japanese ceramics refer to Japanese periods when discussing periods of production. These periods are based on the years of the current Emperor's reign. Those that concern us are:

NAME OF PERIOD	EMPEROR	YEARS
Meiji Period	Mutsuhito	1867 – 1912
Taisho Period	Yoshihito	1912 – 1926
Showa Period	Hirohito	1926 – 1989

As Made in Japan collectors, our main period is Showa, with a little Taisho thrown in for good measure. So, we can honestly and accurately say we specialize in Japanese ceramics of the Showa period. Memorize this phrase and try it out on your unenlightened friends who thought you just collected that Japanese junk!!

A NEW CLEANING TIP

Carol Carder, an antiques dealer, advised me to try peanut butter to remove gummy price sticker residue. I was desperate to clean up two lovely pieces with old, fossilized tape. I daubed the peanut butter right on top of the tape and covered the pieces with plastic wrap so they wouldn't draw insects. At the end of the day, I could see a slight improvement. So I put on fresh peanut butter and let the pieces sit covered on the counter for a week. By then the peanut butter had dried out, and one of the pieces was clear enough to wash. The second one was still corroded, so I left it for another week, then still another. Finally, the tape residue was able to be lifted off by patting it with my finger. The peanut butter did not stain the pieces, and it did ultimately melt away those awful tapes. (Just so you know — at our house we prefer the crunchy style that has no sugar or other added ingredients, so that's what I used. If I were buying it just for cleaning, I would get creamy because the crunchy was a little messy, and I had to be extra careful not to scratch the luster.)

≥ The Marks ≤

There were thousands of different marks used on Made in Japan ceramics over the years. Manufacturers, exporters, importers, and retail sellers could mark their pieces however they preferred, as long as they included "Japan" or "Made in Japan." Because there are so many Marks and Labels, we are limiting ourselves to the more than 112 on pieces in this book, and in Book 1. If your piece has a Mark that is different than one shown here, that does not make it rare just because it's not "in the book." It simply means that it was not used on a piece that we happened to photograph!

Mark 1

Mark 2

Mark 3

Mark 3A

Mark 4

Mark 5

Mark 6

Mark 7

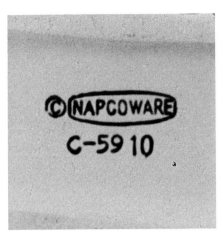

Mark 8

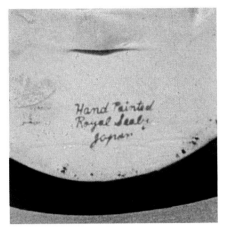

Mark 9

Mark 10

Mark 11

Mark 12

Mark 12A

Mark 13

Mark 14

Mark 15

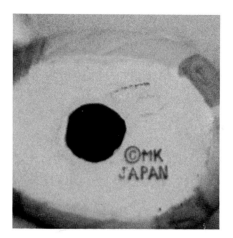

Mark 16

Mark 17

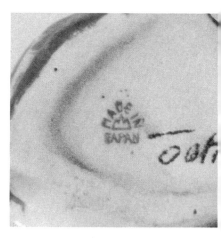

Mark 18

Mark 19

Mark 20

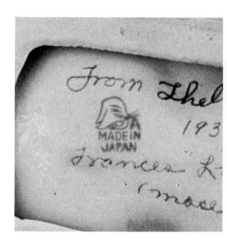

Mark 21

Mark 21A

Mark 22

Mark 23

Mark 23A

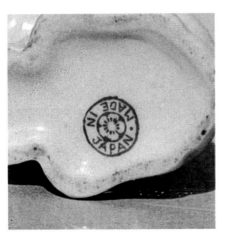

Mark 24

Mark 25

Mark 26

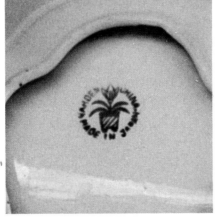

Mark 27

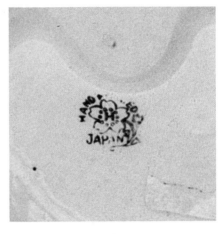

Mark 28

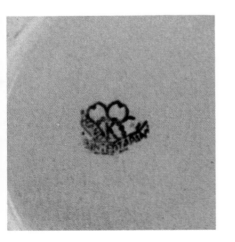

Mark 29

Mark 30

Mark 30A

Mark 31

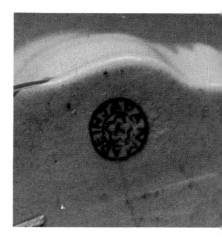

Mark 32

Mark 32A

Mark 33

Mark 34

Mark 35

Mark 36

Mark 37

Mark 38

Mark 39

Mark 40

Mark 41

Mark 42

Mark 43

Mark 43A

Mark 44

Mark 45

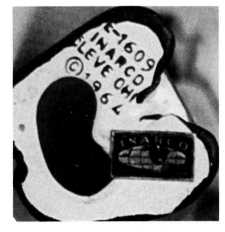

Mark 46

Mark 47

Mark 48

Mark 49

Mark 50

Mark 51

Mark 51A

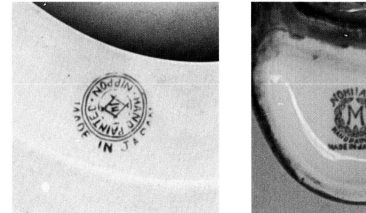

Mark 52

Mark 53

Mark 54

Mark 55

Mark 56

Mark 57

Mark 58

Mark 59

Mark 60

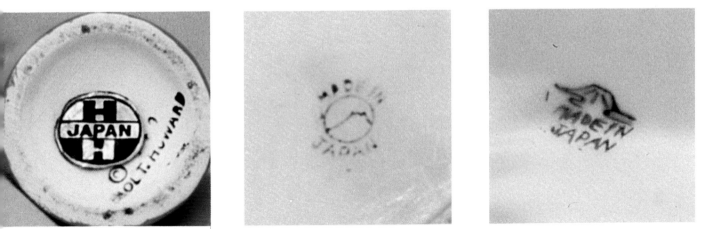

Mark 61

Mark 62

Mark 63

Mark 64

Mark 65

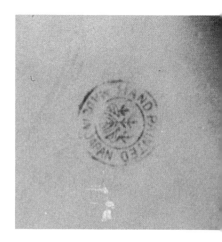

Mark 66

Mark 66A

Mark 66B

Mark 66C

Mark 67

Mark 68

Mark 69

Mark 70

Mark 71

Mark 72

Mark 73

Mark 74

Mark 75

Mark 76

Mark 77

Mark 78

Mark 79

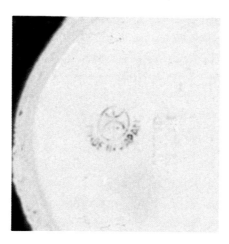

Mark 80

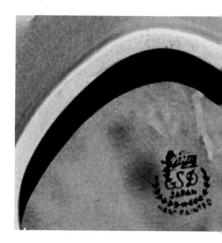

Mark 81

Mark 81 (close-up)

Mark 82

Mark 83

Mark 84

Mark 85

Mark 86

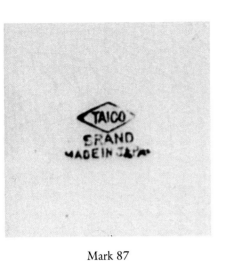

Mark 87

Mark 88

Mark 89

Mark 90

Mark 91

Mark 92

Mark 93

Mark 94

Mark 95

Mark 96

Mark 97

Mark 98

Mark 99

Mark 100

Mark 101

Mark 102

Mark 103

Mark 104

Mark 105

Mark 106

Mark 107

Mark 108

Mark 109

Mark 110

Mark 111

Mark 112

◁ The Collectibles ▷

In the captions, pieces are listed from left to right. All measurements are for height, unless otherwise indicated, and have been rounded off to the nearest quarter-inch. Even though the color of the ink on the backstamp is not an indication of age, it is included anyway, where possible.

The naming of pieces' functions is based on research and direct knowledge, or comparison with similar objects. However what the actual function was meant to be is often lost to us today. Also, items were sold with multiple functions, depending on what was desired by consumers at a given time. So the piece that is a nut cup to me might be a salt dip to you and a plant rooter to your grandma. Since there are no "function police" to arrest us for misnaming, we'll just have to agree that if it's our piece, we can call it whatever we wish!

Some items are noted as Akiyama pieces. The Akiyama family had Oriental gift stores in Portland, Oregon, from the 1920s until 1942. They were interned for the duration of World War II, so they stored the remaining stock in the basement of their house. It stayed there until 1987, when Hanji Akiyama, their son, sold the house and placed the pieces in a local antique mall.

Other pieces are noted as shown in the Sears & Roebuck, Larkin, or Butler Brothers catalogs.

Luckily, a few pieces had the date they were received inscribed on them, and others have been in their owners' families since their purchase; these are so noted.

Some pieces have natural handles. In the old catalogs they were referred to as reed, split bamboo, cane, and wicker. Since they all appear to be the same, or at least very similar, they will all be called "reed" in this book. If a piece has small, round holes, such as the bowl on page 31, it was probably meant to have a reed handle. If the holes are another shape, it may or may not have come with a handle. The cake plate on page 127 has triangular holes, and it was sold without a handle.

The main types of glazes used on Made in Japan ceramics are:

Luster (metallic or pearly-looking overglaze). The older catalogs refer to the goldish-tan color as "tan." The more orange color is called "amber." The only luster that is truly gold is the one that actually looks like the color of golden jewelry. A WARNING — Mr. Keishi Suzuki of the Noritake Company reminds us that old luster glazes can have a high lead content. This means that if we actually use our luster-glazed pieces, we should be careful not to serve acidic foods in them, or allow moist foods to sit in them too long.

Shiny (glossy).

Matte (flat, opaque with no shine).

Semi-matte (opaque with some shine).

Crackle (glaze that is deliberately designed to have cracks in it.) Sometimes glazes are crazed due to age or water damage and may appear to be crackled, but the true crackle glaze will have uniform crackling. Often nicer crackle pieces had black or colored stains rubbed into the cracks to accentuate them.

Bisque (these pieces usually have no glaze at all over all or most of the piece.) They often have accent staining or painting but sometimes they do have areas of fired glaze.

Measurements are for height, unless otherwise noted.

Prices are shown in ranges to reflect the lower and higher-priced regions of the country. If there are sets pictured, prices are for the set unless noted otherwise.

This book, along with Volume 1, gives an overview of as many types as possible of the hundreds of thousands of Made in Japan ceramic collectibles made over the years.

⚓ Art Deco ⚓

Based on natural and geometric forms, Art Deco was the distinctive style of the 1920s, 1930s, and early 1940s. Deco pieces sometimes have repeated patterns of flowers, fruits, or figures, or they may have only a panel with an Art Deco motif. They may be decorated entirely with geometric shapes, or the shape of the piece itself may be Art Deco.

Plate 2. Basket in multicolored luster glazes with floral motif, 6¼" wide, Black Mark #1, $45.00 – $68.00.

Plate 1. Cat bank in blue shiny glaze, 4¼", Black Mark #1, $15.00 – $25.00.

Plate 3. Basket in tan, yellow, and blue luster glazes with multicolored Art Deco lady motif, 8½" wide, Black Mark #1, $48.00 – $75.00.

Plate 4. Biscuit barrel in cream glaze with airbrushed blue and tan Art Deco motif, 6", Black Mark #88, $45.00 – $75.00.

Plate 5. Card suit biscuit barrel in yellow and multicolored shiny glazes, 5½", Red Mark #25, $45.00 – $75.00.

Plate 6. (A) Scenic biscuit barrel in multicolored luster glazes with enameling, 6", Red Mark #25, $45.00 – $65.00. (B) Pagoda biscuit barrel in multicolored luster glazes, pictured in the 1932 Sears & Roebuck Catalog as a cookie jar for $1.00, 8¼", Black Mark #1, $45.00 – $65.00.

Plate 7. Sailboat bookends in blue and multicolored shiny glazes, 4¾", Red Mark #2, $25.00 – $45.00.

Plate 8. Rare console bowl in orange and blue semi-matte glazes, 9½" wide, Blue Mark #77, $28.00 – $55.00.

Plate 9. Noritake oval bowl in multicolored semi-matte glazes, 8¼" wide, Red Mark #53, $20.00 – $55.00.

Plate 10. Noritake oval bowl in multicolored luster glazes, 7½" wide, Red Mark #53, $27.00 – $57.00.

Plate 11. Bowl in multicolored luster glazes with blue cat handle, 7" wide, Red Mark #1, $25.00 – $50.00.

Plate 12. Goldcastle bowl in multicolored luster glazes with orange cat handle, 7¼" wide, Red Mark #43, $25.00 – $50.00.

Detail of cat handles.

Plate 13. Bowl with butterflies in blue luster and multicolored matte glazes, 7" wide, Red Mark #56, $35.00 – $55.00.

Plate 14. Bowl with lady in tan and multicolored luster and matte glazes, 8¼" wide, Red Mark #56, $25.00 – $50.00.

Plate 15. Two Meito bowls in multicolored luster glazes. (A) 8", Red & Green Mark #64, $20.00 – $45.00. (B) 6", Red & Green Mark #64, $20.00 – $45.00.

Plate 16. Bowl in multicolored luster glazes with reed handle, 8" wide, Red Mark #25, $15.00 – $35.00.

Plate 17. Noritake nappy bowl in silver, tan, and multicolored luster glazes, 5½" wide, Red Mark #53, $18.00 – $35.00.

Plate 18. Meito candlestick in tan luster glaze with multicolored floral medallion, 8¼", Red & Green Mark #64, $30.00 – $50.00.

Plate 19. Meito candlestick in blue semi-matte glaze with multicolored bird motif, 9¾", Red & Green Mark #64, $30.00 – $50.00.

Plate 20. Rare cat covered candy dish in tan and blue luster, 6¾", Red Mark #1, $75.00 – $125.00.

Plate 21. Rare cat candy dish in multicolored luster glazes, pictured in a pre-World War II Butler Bros. Catalog for $.65 wholesale/$1.00 – $1.50 retail, 4¼", Black Mark #1, $25.00 – $50.00.

Plate 22. Goldcastle cigarette holder in yellow luster glaze and multicolored shiny glazes, 3¼", Red Mark #43, $20.00 – $30.00.

Plate 23. (A) Clown cigarette holder (the head is the lid) in multicolored luster glazes, 5", Black Mark #1, $35.00 – $75.00. (B) Match holder and ashtray in multicolored luster & shiny glazes, 6", Red Mark #25, $28.00 – $50.00.

Plate 25. Cigarette box in green and white shiny glazes with dog, 3", Red Mark #25, $20.00 – $35.00.

Plate 24. Cat cigarette box in multicolored luster glazes, 3¾" wide, Black Mark #1, $30.00 – $50.00.

Plate 26. Stacking cream and sugar in white shiny glaze with multicolored motif (probably came stacked with a teapot), 5", Red Mark #1, $22.00 – $32.00.

Plate 27. (A) Lemon server in blue and multicolored luster glazes, 5¾", Black Mark #1, $20.00 – $35.00. (B) Lemon server in tan and multicolored luster glazes, 5¾", Red Mark #1, $20.00 – $35.00.

Plate 28. Lemon server in multicolored luster with silver accents, pictured in the 1932 Sears & Roebuck Catalog with a bone fork for $.39, 5¾", Red Mark #66, $20.00 – $35.00.

Plate 29. Noritake lemon server in tan and multicolored luster glazes, 5¾", Red Mark #53, $25.00 – $50.00.

Plate 30. Noritake lemon server in multicolored shiny glazes, 5½", Red Mark #53, $25.00 – $50.00.

Plate 31. Marmalade set in blue and multicolored luster glazes, pictured in the 1932 Sears & Roebuck Catalog for $.59 with different decoration, 5½" tall, pot and plate Red Mark #24, $55.00 – $85.00.

Plate 32. Goldcastle mayonnaise set in ivory luster with multicolored motif, plate 6" wide, plate and bowl Black Mark #43, $35.00 – $65.00.

Plate 33. Rare pitcher in multicolored luster and orange shiny glazes, 8½", Red Mark #1, $50.00 – $110.00.

Plate 34. (A) Pitcher in multicolored luster and shiny glazes, 5", Black Mark #10, $35.00 – 75.00. (B) Pitcher in multicolored luster glazes with pagoda scene, 6", Black Mark #1, $25.00 – $55.00.

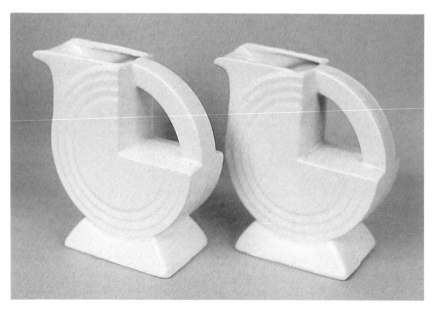

Plate 35. Pair of pitchers in white semi-matte glaze, 5¼", Black Mark #1, $15.00 – $25.00 each.

Plate 36. Teapot, creamer, and sugar in black and white luster glazes, 8" tall, all Red Mark #1, set $75.00 – $125.00.

Plate 37. Teapot, creamer, sugar, and tray in blue luster glaze with multicolored floral motif, pot 6¼", all Red Mark #1, set $80.00 – $125.00.

Plate 38. Teapot, creamer, sugar, and tray in blue and multicolored luster glazes and enameling, pot 5", all Red Mark #25, set $80.00 – $125.00.

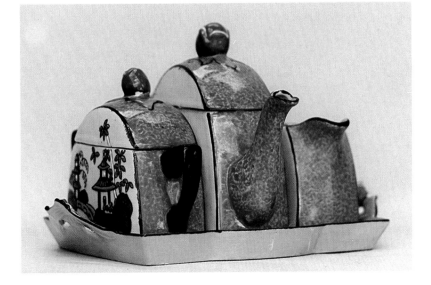

Plate 39. Teapot, creamer, an
sugar in blue and multicolore
luster glazes, pot 5" with Re
Mark #1, creamer and sugar n
Mark, set $65.00 – $100.00.

Plate 40. Sunburst teapot,
creamer, and sugar in blue,
orange, and yellow semi-matte
glazes, pot 6¾", all Red Mark
#25, set $75.00 – $125.00.

Plate 41. (A) Teapot and
hot water set with pagod
and bridge in multicolore
luster glazes, pot 5", both
Red Mark #56, set $45.00
– $85.00. (B) Teapot and
hot water set with multicol
ored floral and stripe motif
pot 5", both Red Mark
#25, set $45.00 – $85.00.

Plate 42. Teapot and hot water set with multicolored stripe motif, same shape as those on page 38 but showing front view, pot 5", both Red Mark #25, set $45.00 – $85.00.

Plate 43. (A) Teapot on tile in orange and white shiny glaze, pot 4½", Red Mark #48, set $38.00 – $62.00. (B) Teapot in orange and white shiny glaze, pot 7", Red Mark #24, $32.00 – $47.00.

Plate 44. Teapot on tile in blue and multicolored luster glazes, pot 7¾", Red Mark #25, set $38.00 – $62.00.

Plate 45. (A) Teapot on tile with green oil spot glaze and multicolored floral motif and enameling, pot 7½", Red Mark #25, $38.00 – $62.00. (B) Teapot on tile in yellow luster with multicolored floral motif and enameling, pot 7½", Red Mark #25, set $38.00 – $62.00.

Plate 46. (A) Teapot in cream and green crackle glaze with multicolored floral motif, 6¾", Red Mark #25, $33.00 – $60.00. (B) Teapot in green and cream crackle glaze with multicolored floral motif, Red Mark #25, $33.00 – $60.00.

Plate 47. (A) Teapot in orange shiny glaze with yellow shamrocks, 6", Black Mark #30, $32.00 – $47.00. (B) Teapot in orange shiny and yellow luster glaze, 5", Mark obscured, $32.00 – $47.00.

Plate 48. (A) Teapot in orange, green, and black shiny glaze, 6½", Red Mark #25, $32.00 – $47.00. (B) Teapot in orange and multicolored luster glazes, 6½", Black Mark #21, $32.00 – $47.00.

Plate 49. (A) Teapot in blue and multicolored luster glazes with wave motif, 7", Red Mark #1, $32.00 – $47.00. (B) Teapot in blue and tan luster glazes with multicolored floral motif, 5", Black Mark #1, $32.00 – 47.00.

Plate 50. (A) Teapot in aqua and multicolored luster glazes, 4½", Black Mark #1, $32.00 – $47.00. (B) Goldcastle teapot in aqua and multicolored luster glazes, 6½", Black Mark #43, $32.00 – $47.00.

Plate 51. Teapot with matching salt and sugar. (A) Salt in white shiny glaze with multicolored floral motif, 2¾" no Mark, $6.00 – $10.00. (B) Teapot, 4½", Red Mark #66C, $32.00 – $50.00. (C) Sugar, 4½", Red Mark #66C, $8.00 – $15.00.

Plate 52. (A) Cruet set in white shiny glaze with multicolored floral motif, matching the teapot above, 7", Red Mark #66C, set $20.00 – $30.00. (B) Drippings jar, 5½", Red Mark #66C and number "12," $15.00 – $25.00.

Plate 53. Noritake tray in multicolored luster glazes, 14½" wide, Green Mark #26, $55.00 – $110.00.

Plate 54. Tray in amber and multicolored luster glazes, 10½" wide, Black Mark #1, $24.00 – $43.00.

Plate 56. Goldcastle vase in multicolored luster glazes with geometric motif, 7¼", Black Mark #43, $35.00 – $55.00.

Plate 55. Kinkozan vase in gold luster and multicolored shiny glazes, a pre-World War II piece, 9¾", Red Mark #49, $75.00 – $125.00.

Plate 57. Vase in yellow luster with multicolored luster glazes and floral motif, 7", Black Mark #1, $40.00 – $55.00.

Plate 58. Basket-shaped vase in blue and tan luster glazes, 3¾", Red Mark #25, $20.00 – $45.00.

Plate 59. Vase in tan luster glaze with multicolored floral motif, 5½", Red Mark #1, $30.00 – $50.00.

Plate 60. (A) Vase in opalescent luster glaze with multicolored luster floral motif and accents, 7¾", Red Mark #12, $26.00 – $38.00. (B) Handled vase in white shiny glaze with blue luster and multicolored floral motif, 5", Red Mark #20, $25.00 – $35.00.

Plate 61. (A) Goldcastle handled vase in multicolored shiny glazes, 5½", Red Mark #44, $28.00 – $43.00. (B) Vase in purple and multicolored matte glazes, 5¼", Black Mark #32, $25.00 – $32.00.

Plate 62. (A) Cat vase in gold luster glaze and multicolored matte glazes, 3¼", Red Mark #1, $15.00 – $27.00. (B) Cat vase in blue shiny glaze with black figure, 4¼", no Mark, $18.00 – $29.00.

Plate 63. Cat vase in multicolored shiny and semi-matte glazes, 5¼", Red Mark #1, $20.00 – $45.00.

Plate 64. (A) Geometric vase in cream and multicolored shiny glazes, pictured in the 1929 Sears & Roebuck Catalog for $.59, 7¼", Black Mark #1, $22.00 – $36.00. (B) Handled geometric vase in blue and white matte glazes, 5¾", Black Mark #1, $15.00 – $28.00.

Plate 65. (A) Vase in multicolored luster glazes with floral motif, pictured in a pre-World War II Butler Bros. Catalog in an assortment of pieces for $4.00 a dozen, 5", Red Mark #1, $25.00 – $45.00. (B) Vase in yellow crackle glaze with multicolored embossed floral motif, pictured in the 1929 Sears & Roebuck Catalog for $.59, 7", Black Mark #1, $22.00 – $36.00.

Plate 66. Vase with sailboat motif in blue and white shiny glazes, 7¾", Black Mark #1, $10.00 – $25.00.

Plate 67. (A) Vase in cream shiny glaze with parrot motif hand painted by an American hobbyist "on the blank," inscribed "Pearl Deegan Xmas 1925," 7¼", Blind Mark #2, $25.00 – $40.00. (B) Vase in orange and cream shiny glazes, 7¼", Black Mark #1, $23.00 – $38.00.

Plate 68. (A) Tulip-shaped vase in multicolored shiny glazes, 6", Black Mark #1, $25.00 – $42.00. (B) Goldcastle vase in yellow and multicolored shiny glazes, 6", Red Mark #44, $25.00 – $48.00.

Plate 69. Vase in pink crackle glaze with multicolored floral motif, 7¼", Black Mark #1, $28.00 – $48.00.

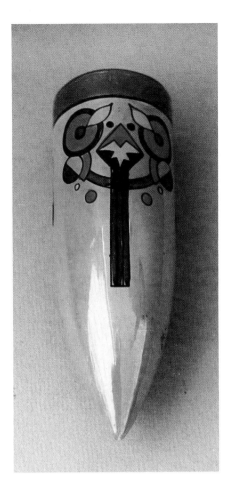

Plate 70. Goldcastle wall pocket in multicolored luster glazes, 7¼", Red Mark #44, $29.00 – $41.00.

Plate 71. Wall pocket in red and multicolored luster glazes, 6½", Red Mark #11, $27.00 – $38.00.

◁ Ashtrays ▷

Ashtrays continue to be among the more plentiful Made in Japan collectibles, and their varied shapes and sizes keep them interesting to collectors. They often came in sets of four, frequently with the four card suits. With the card suit motifs, they were popular bridge prizes. Finding a set in the original box adds 10 – 15% to the value.

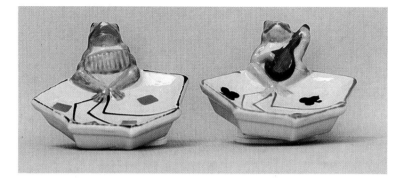

Plate 72. Two frog card suit ashtrays in green and multicolored shiny glazes, 1¾" wide, (A) Blue Mark #1; (B) Black Mark #1; $13.00 – $23.00 each.

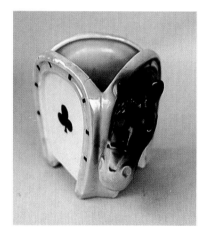

Plate 73. Card suit ashtray with horseshoe motif in tan luster glaze and multicolored shiny glazed horse, 4", Red Mark #38, Blind Mark #2, $15.00 – $32.00.

Plate 74. Two card suit ashtrays in orange and multicolored semi-matte glazes, (A) 2½", Red Mark #1; (B) 2¾", Black Mark #1; $18.00 – $28.00 each.

Plate 75. Ashtray in multicolored shiny glazes, inscribed "FUKUYA and CO JEWELRY STORE, MOTOMACHI STREET, YOKOHAMA, TEL. 2-3693," 6" wide, Multicolored Mark #75 (a post-WWII mark of the Narumi company, which was formerly the Meito China Company), $8.00 – $15.00.

Plate 76. Two contrasting ashtrays. (A) 1950s "Moderne" style, 5" wide, Red Mark #23, $15.00 – $22.00. (B) 1930s style in multicolored luster with blown-out berry motif, 4½" wide, Red Mark #20, $10.00 – $18.00.

Plate 77. Set of four rare dog ashtrays with matchbook holders in amber and multicolored luster glazes with black scenic motif, 3¾", Black Mark #1, set of four, $80.00 – $120.00.

Plate 78. Three pieces showing use of the same figure in different ways. (A) Ashtray, 2½" $8.00 – $18.00. (B) Figurine, 4¼", $12.00 – $21.00. (C) Cigarette or toothpick holder, 2½", $10.00 – $18.00. All Black Mark #1.

Plate 79. (A) Elephant ashtray in green and blue shiny glaze, 2½", Black Mark #1, $20.00 – $32.00. (B) Dog ashtray in orange semi-matte glaze, 2½", Red Mark #1, $20.00 – $32.00.

Plate 80. (A) Dog ashtray with cigarette or match holder in green and multicolored semi-matte glazes, 2½", Red Mark #1, $20.00 – $35.00. (B) Bird ashtray in tan, blue, and multicolored luster glazes, 2½", Black Mark #1, $15.00 – $25.00.

Plate 81. (A) Cat ashtray with snuffers in blue luster glaze, 4¼", Red Mark #1, $16.00 – $32.00. (B) Cat ashtray with snuffers on sides and in cat's head in green and multicolored luster glazes, 3½", Black Mark #1 and Blind Mark #1, $16.00 – $32.00.

Plate 82. (A) Monkey ashtray with snuffers in aqua luster glaze with multicolored figure, 2", Red Mark #1 and Blind Mark #1, $11.00 – $22.00. (B) Dog ashtray in multicolored luster glazes, 3", Red Mark #1, $12.00 – $22.00.

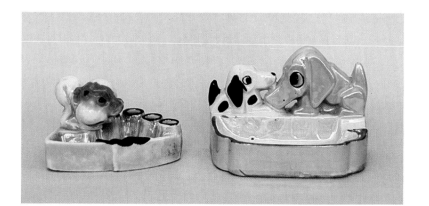

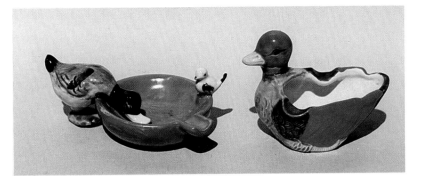

Plate 83. (A) Duck and bird ashtray in green and multicolored shiny glazes, 2", Black Mark #1, $18.00 – $28.00. (B) Duck ashtray in red, green, and blue semi-matte glazes, 3¼", Red Mark #2, $18.00 – $28.00.

Plate 84. Frog ashtray in yellow luster and multicolored shiny glazes, 2½", Black Mark #1, $18.00 – $28.00.

Plate 85. Cat ashtray in black shiny glaze on brown clay body, 4¾", no Mark, $12.00 – $22.00.

Plate 86. (A) Cat ashtray in black shiny glaze on brown body, 3¾", no Mark but inscribed "109," $12.00 – $18.00. (B) Pipe ashtray in black shiny glaze on brown body, 8¾" wide, Blind Mark #1, $12.00 – $18.00.

Plate 87. Hunt scene ashtray in amber luster glaze with multicolored figure and label "Rockaway Beach," 3½", Black Mark #38 and Blind Mark #1, $22.00 – $32.00.

Plate 88. Hunt scene ashtray with Kakiemon-like decorations in white and multicolored shiny glazes, 4", Black Mark #1 and Blind Mark #1 with "D2071," $22.00 – $32.00.

Plate 89. Clown ashtray with snuffers in white shiny and multicolored semi-matte glazes, 5¼", Blue Mark #1, $38.00 – $53.00.

Plate 90. Sailor couple ashtray in tan luster and multicolored shiny glazes, 4", Black Mark #1, $30.00 – $60.00.

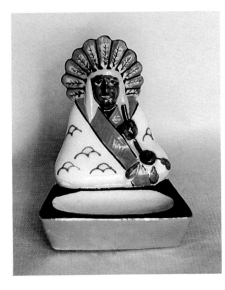

Plate 92. Indian on canoe ashtray or pin tray in tan and blue luster glazes with multicolored matte figure, 3", Black Mark #56, $30.00 – $60.00.

Plate 91. Indian ashtray or pin tray in blue and multicolored luster glazes, 4½", Black Mark #56, $30.00 – $60.00.

Plate 93. Toddler with turtle ashtray in multicolored shiny glazes, 2¾", Red Mark #2, $18.00 – $28.00.

⚞ Banks ⚟

How does one tell if a piece is a bank or a razor safe? Both have slots. If it has a hole (or a break-out dimple) to remove coins, it is probably a bank. If not, it is difficult to tell. Razor safes usually had no removal hole and were fairly small and heavy and they were not childish looking.

Plate 94. Bank in gray opalescent luster glaze, 4½", Red Mark #2, $15.00 – $25.00.

Plate 95. Dog bank in multicolored shiny glazes, 5", Black Mark #1, $15.00 – $25.00.

Plate 96. Three dog banks in multicolored shiny glazes. (A) 4¾", Red Mark #1, $15.00 – $23.00. (B) 4¾", Red Mark #1, $15.00 – $23.00. (C) 3¼", Black Mark #1, $12.00 – $18.00.

Plate 97. Pair of post-World War II friar banks in brown and multicolored shiny glazes, 5¼"; (A) Black Mark #78, with paper label "JAPAN"; (B) Black Mark #78 only; $8.00 – $18.00 each.

Plate 98. Hummel-type girl with umbrella bank inscribed "SAVE FOR RAINY DAY" in red and multicolored matte glazes, Black Mark #2, 5¼", $15.00 – $22.00.

⚐ Bells ⚐

Bells are popular collectibles both with and without the clappers. In fact, a missing clapper does not seem to affect the value of the piece much, if any.

Plate 99. Colonial lady bell in multicolored matte glazes with label "SEATTLE WASH," 4¾", Black Mark #1, $18.00 – $25.00.

Plate 100. (A) Lady with purse bell in multicolored shiny and matte glazes, 3½", Black Mark #1, $8.00 – $16.00. (B) Santa bell, twice-traveled because he was exported from Japan to the U.S.A., then shipped back to Japan, where he was purchased and given to me by a friend, 2¼", Red Mark #2, $5.00 – $12.00.

Plate 101. (A) Man bell in orange and multicolored shiny glazes, 4¼", Red Mark #66A, $20.00 – $45.00. (B) Lady bell in lavender and multicolored shiny glazes, 4½", Red Mark #1, $20.00 – $45.00.

Plate 102. (A) Flower lady bell in green and multicolored semi-matte glazes, 4½", Black Mark #1, $10.00 – $18.00. (B) Maid bell in multicolored semi-matte glazes, 4¾", $10.00 – $18.00.

Plate 103. (A) Lady with flower bell in green and orange semi-matte glazes, 4½", Red Mark #2 and Blind Mark #2, $10.00 – $18.00. (B) Maruyama lady bell in yellow luster glaze, 4¾", Red Mark #65, $20.00 – $30.00.

⚰ Bookends ⚰

Collectors seem to collect both in pairs or singles, and they don't seem to mind whether they have been filled with plaster or not, so bookends hold their value regardless.

Plate 104. Maruyama dog bookends in multicolored shiny glazes with green oil spot bases, 5", Red Mark #1 and Blind Mark #65, pair, $25.00 – $36.00.

Plate 105. Scottie dog bookends in yellow and multicolored luster glazes, 6½", Red Mark #1, $25.00 – $40.00.

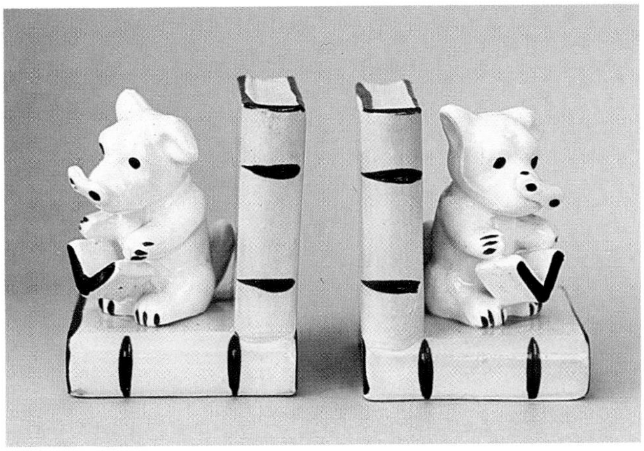

Plate 106. Scottie dog with spectacles bookends in blue and white shiny glazes, 4", Black Mark #1, $18.00 – $28.00.

Plate 107. Poodle bookends in black shiny glaze on brown clay body, 6", Gold Mark #2, $12.00 – $28.00.

Plate 108. Cat bookends in black shiny glaze on brown clay body, 5¾", Gold Mark #2, $12.00 – $28.00.

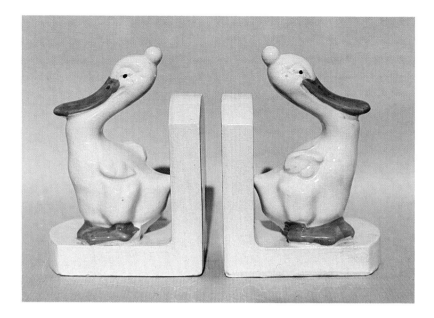

Plate 109. Pelican bookends in cream and multicolored matte glazes inscribed "TO ANGEL MARCH 17, 1941," 6", Black Mark #1, $25.00 – $50.00.

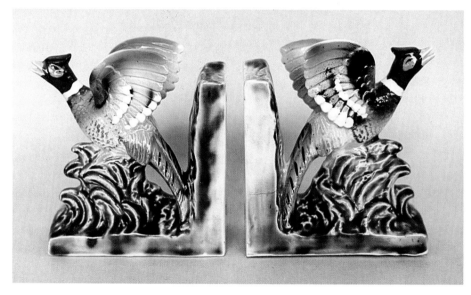

Plate 110. Bird post-World War II bookends in multicolored shiny glazes, 5", Label #108, $12.00 – $22.00.

Plate 111. Boy with accordion and girl with umbrella bookends in multicolored shiny glazes, 6¼", Black Mark #79, $28.00 – $55.00.

Plate 112. Boy and girl bookends in black and white shiny glazes, 6", Black Mark #1, $24.00 – $34.00.

Plate 113. Oriental figure bookends or incense burners in tan and multicolored luster glazes, 5½", Blind Mark #1, $35.00 – $55.00 (this pair was used as bookends — they are filled, sealed, and come as a set).

Plate 114. Mexican figure bookends in green and multicolored luster and shiny glazes, 4¼", Black Mark #2, $25.00 – $45.00.

⚞ Bowls ⚟

Included here are serving bowls of all types, as well as flower bowls.

Plate 115. Noritake bowl in blue and tan luster glazes, 9¼" wide, Green Mark #53, $25.00 – $65.00.

Plate 116. Swan scenic serving bowl in tan luster and multicolored shiny glazes, 7½" wide, Green Mark #36, $25.00 – $38.00.

Plate 117. Goldcastle flower bowl in amber luster with multicolored fruit motif, pictured in the 1927 Sears & Roebuck Catalog in different colors for $1.25, 8½" wide, Red Mark #43, $35.00 – $55.00.

Plate 118. Centerpiece bowl with attached candle- holders in blue luster with orange and black semi-matte glazes, 8¾" wide, no Mark, $25.00 – $45.00.

Plate 119. Bowl with sprigged-on flowers and butterflies in blue and multicolored luster glazes, 6½" wide, Red Mark #20, $30.00 – $45.00.

Plate 120. Scenic bowl with sprigged-on flower handle in blue, tan, and multicolored luster glazes (the blank is the same as a Noritake piece), 7¼" wide, Red Mark #25, $20.00 – $35.00.

Plate 121. Bowl in Majolica-type blue and multicolored shiny glazes, 9" wide, Black Mark #1, $24.00 – $38.00.

Plate 122. Frog and duck bowl in green and cream shiny glazes (similar to Czech Peasant Ware), 9¼" wide, Blind Mark #1, $30.00 – $55.00.

Plate 123. Leaf bowl in multicolored green shiny glazes, 7¾" wide, Red Mark #3A, $1.00 – $5.00.

Plate 124. Leaf bowl in multicolored semi-matte glaze, 6¼" wide, Gold Mark #57, $1.00 – $5.00.

Plate 125. Clown bowl in multicolored shiny glazes, 10" long, Black Mark #2, $15.00 – $25.00.

⚞ Cake Plates ⚟

Cake serving plates were sold separately or in sets with six 6" – 7" plates. The smaller plates were sold separately as sets also. This makes it a challenge to assemble a matching set!

Plate 126. Cake set in aqua and multicolored luster glazes, pictured in the 1927 Sears & Roebuck Catalog with a different motif for $3.45, cake plate 9¾" wide all Black Mark #52, $28.00 – $52.00.

Plate 127. Noritake handled cake or sandwich tray in tan luster with multicolored scenic footbridge motif, 7½" wide, Green Mark #53, $25.00 – $60.00.

Plate 128. Noritake cake plate with multicolored scenic motif, 7½" wide, Green Mark #53, $25.00 – $60.00.

⚐ Calico Animals ⚐

Characteristics of calico animals are white shiny base glaze, spots, stripes, or splashes of bright colors, and relatively humorous and unsophisticated figures.

Plate 129. Calico elephant card suit ashtray, 2¼", Mark obscured, $17.00 – $27.00.

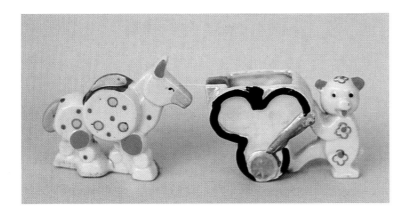

Plate 130. (A) Calico disc horse pincushion, 3", Red Mark #1, $26.00 – $36.00. (B) Calico cat with wheelbarrow, card suit ashtray, 2¼", Black Mark #2, $15.00 – $20.00.

Plate 131. (A) Goldcastle calico animal ashtray with snuffers, 3", Black Mark #43, $15.00 – $22.00. (B) Calico animal ashtray with snuffers on sides and in head, 3¼", Blind Mark #1 with Japanese characters, $20.00 – $28.00.

Plate 132. Calico cat ashtray with Japanese mountain scene, 2½", Black Mark #1, $18.00 – $29.00.

Plate 133. Calico calendar without day/date/month cards, 2½", Black Mark #1, $22.00 – $35.00.

Plate 134. Three calico elephant pincushions. (A) 3¼", Black Mark #1 (spots have been rubbed off), $6.00 – $10.00. (B) 3", Black Mark #1, $17.00 – $27.00. (C) 2¾", Black Mark #1, $17.00 – $27.00.

Plate 135. Two calico animal pincushions. (A) Cat, 3", Red Mark #1, $17.00 – $27.00. (B) Dog, 3¼", Black Mark #1, $17.00 – $27.00.

Plate 136. Calico salt and pepper shakers. (A) Black Mark #2, and (D) Red Mark #1, $18.00 – $20.00. (B) and (C) Calico muffineer set, 6¾", Black Mark #1, $50.00 – $86.00.

Plate 137. Calico cat salt and pepper, 3½", Red Mark #2, $18.00 – $20.00.

Plate 138. Calico dog toothbrush holder, 3¾", Black Mark #1, $55.00 – $70.00.

Plate 139. Calico hippo vase, 3¼", Black Mark #2, $14.00 – $25.00.

⚞ Candleholders ⚟

The popular conception seems to be that a candleholder with a handle is called a chamberstick whether or not it has saucer or bowl to catch the wax.

Plate 140. Pair of bird candlesticks in blue and multicolored semi-matte glazes, 5½", Black Mark #1, pair $100.00 – $150.00.

Plate 141. Pair of candlesticks in multicolored shiny glazes, a pre-WWII set from the Akiyama store, (A) 7¼", (B) 7½", both Black Mark #2 with Japanese characters, pair, $125.00 – $150.00.

Plate 142. Pair of candlesticks in amber and cream mottled luster glazes, 6¼", Red Mark #2, pair, $25.00 – $45.00.

Plate 143. Imitation Gouda-style grouping (Gouda Ware has been made in Holland since the 1600s). (A) and (C) Mini vases, 2½", Black Mark #1, $8.00 – $15.00 each. (B) Candlestick, 3¾", Black Mark #1, $12.00 – $18.00.

Plate 144. Chamberstick in green, black, and red shiny glazes, 2½", Red Mark #20, $12.00 – $18.00.

Plate 145. Chamberstick style candleholder in yellow and multicolored shiny glazes, 4½", Black Mark #1, $30.00 – $45.00.

Plate 146. Chamberstick in multicolored rustic crackle glazes, 6", Red Mark #25, $25.00 – $48.00.

ᗙ Candy Dishes ᗚ

As with so many Japanese shapes, dishes that today we would call candies were sold with multiple names. This makes it a challenge to separate the powder box from the cigarette jar from the candy dish!

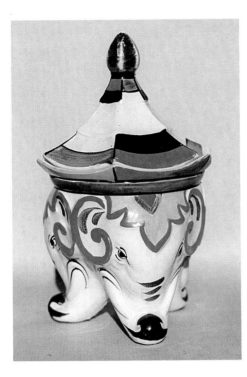

Plate 147. Rare elephant covered candy in white and multicolored shiny glazes, 8¾", Red Mark #67, $50.00 – $100.00.

Plate 148. Candy box in blue luster with multicolored shiny glaze motif, 5½" wide, Red Mark #25, $30.00 – $50.00.

Plate 149. Lotus candy box in multicolored matte glazes, 3¼", Black Mark #1, $30.00 – $50.00.

Plate 151. Very rare Japanese ladies candy dish, 4½", Blue Mark #52, $50.00 – $100.00.

Plate 150. Pierrot covered candy in cream and multicolored shiny glazes, 7", Blind Mark #1, $50.00 – $75.00.

Plate 152. Noritake handled candy dish in tan luster with green and black matte accents, 6½" wide, Green Mark #53, $35.00 – $50.00.

Plate 153. Goldcastle handled candy dish or bonbon basket in ivory and lavender luster glazes with multicolored floral motif, 8¾", Red Mark #43, $18.00 – $29.00.

Plate 154. Handled candy dish or bonbon basket in Majolica-type purple, brown, and multicolored shiny glazes, 4½" wide, Black Mark #80 and Blind Mark #1, $25.00 – $40.00.

Plate 155. Canadian Mountie candy or bonbon dish in brown shiny glaze inscribed "CANADA," 5¾" wide, Black Mark #81 and numbers "ZN7130," $5.00 – $15.00.

⚐ Children's Dishes ⚐

The difference between children's and doll dishes seems to be in the size. One expert explains that children's dishes are large enough for a child to actually use.

Plate 156. Children's dish set in tan luster and multicolored shiny glazes with original box, (a gift to its original owner in the 1930s), all Black Mark #1, $150.00 – $250.00.

Plate 157. "Little Hostess Set" of children's dishes in tan and blue luster glazes with original box, cups, saucers, plates, and teapot Red Mark #1, other pieces no Mark, box labeled "NAGOYA TOY TEA SET No 600 186 (2) Made in Japan," $150.00 – $250.00.

Plate 158. Children's dish set in tan and ivory luster glazes with original box (the Japanese make odd-numbered sets because they consider them to be luckier), all Black Mark #1, box label "Art. No. 7-1191 Made in Japan," $50.00 – $100.00.

Plate 159. Children's dish set in bright colors, platter 6½" wide, all Red Mark #1, except cream and sugar no Mark, $100.00 – $200.00 for the complete set with four plates, cups, and saucers.

Plate 160. Children's teapot, cream, and sugar set in tan luster with multicolored shiny glazes, pot 3¾" Green Mark #1, cream and sugar no Mark, $28.00 – $55.00.

Plate 161. Children's teapot, cream, and sugar set in blue and multicolored luster glazes, pot 4½", no Mark, $28.00 – $55.00.

⚜ Cigarette Items ⚜

Pieces such as those in plate #163 were sold as either cigarette holders, card holders, or vases.

Plate 162. Cigarette set in blue luster glaze, pictured in a pre-World War II Butler Bros. Catalog for $.65 wholesale/$1.00 – $1.50 retail, tray 7" wide, all Red Mark #52, $35.00 – $65.00.

Plate 163. Two cigarette or card holders. (A) Blue and white crackle with multicolored floral motif, 3¼", Black Mark #14 (without patent numbers), $20.00 – $30.00. (B) Blue shiny glaze with pink animal motif, 3", Black Mark #1, $15.00 – $25.00.

Plate 164. Goldcastle dog cigarette box with ashtrays in red shiny glaze, 6", Black Mark #43, $35.00 – $55.00.

Plate 165. Rare elephant cigarette holder or humidor with match holder in multicolored luster glazes, 5½", Black Mark #1, $50.00 – $75.00.

Plate 166. Cigarette box with four flowered side panel hanging ashtrays in multicolored shiny glazes, 4", Red mark #82, $25.00 – $45.00.

Plate 167. (A) Goldcastle cigarette box or humidor with stacking ashtrays in multicolored shiny glazes, 4¾", all Red Mark #44, $25.00 – $45.00. (B) Elephant cigarette box with ashtrays in black shiny glaze on brown body, 4¼", ashtrays no Mark, elephant Blind Mark #2, $20.00 – $35.00.

Plate 168. Two cigarette holders with stacking ashtrays (the ruffles on the necks are the ashtrays). (A) 5", Black Mark #1 and Blind Mark #1, $35.00 – $55.00. (B) 6½", Black Mark #1, $35.00 – $55.00.

Plate 169. Dog with mustache cigarette box in multicolored shiny glazes, 4½", Black Mark #1, $20.00 – $30.00.

Plate 170. Elephant cigarette or candy box in multicolored shiny glazes, 6¾", Red Mark #1, $30.00 – $45.00.

Plate 171. Cigarette box in cream and multicolored shiny glazes, 3¾" wide, Black Mark #1, $18.00 – $28.00.

Plate 172. Cigarette box with dogs in opal luster and multicolored shiny glazes, 3", Black Mark #1, $20.00 – $35.00.

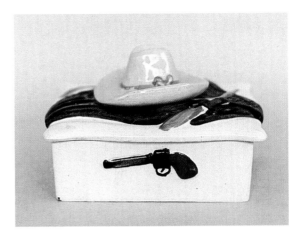

Plate 173. Cowboy cigarette box in multicolored shiny glazes, 5¼" wide, Black Mark #2, $15.00 – $25.00.

Plate 174. Elephant with ashtray and cigarette/match panniers in multicolored luster glazes, 5½", Black Mark #56, $25.00 – $45.00.

Plate 175. Elephant with ashtray and cigarette/match panniers in multicolored mottled shiny glazes, 4½", Black Mark #1, $15.00 – $20.00.

Plate 176. Elephant with cigarette/match panniers in multicolored matte glazes, pictured in the 1929 Sears & Roebuck Catalog as "Combination match and cigarette holder, Taisho China, unique bridge prize" for $.65, 4", no Mark, $25.00 – $45.00.

⚐ Condiment and Salt and Pepper Sets ⚐

The little pots with spoons were usually called mustard pots, but once in a while they would be referred to as mustard or horseradish pots. Some sets came with open toothpick holders.

Plate 177. Condiment set with matching cream and sugar in red, yellow, and green shiny glazes, 7" wide, all Black Mark #2 except tray has no Mark, set $75.00 – $135.00.

Plate 178. Kangaroo condiment set on tray in tan and blue luster glazes, tray 7¼" with Red Mark #52, cruets Red Mark #52, salt, pepper, and mustard no Mark, set $65.00 – $125.00.

Plate 179. Three wise monkeys condiment set in tan and blue luster glazes, 5¾" wide, tray and mustard Red Mark #52, salt and pepper no Mark, set $50.00 – $75.00.

Plate 180. Desert scene condiment set on tray in multicolored shiny glazes, 9¼" wide, cruets, mustard, and tray Red Mark #83, salt and pepper no Mark, set $60.00 – $100.00.

Plate 181. Floral condiment set on tray in multicolored shiny glazes with gold luster, tray 9¼" wide, tray, mustard, and cruets Black Mark #21, salt and pepper Black Mark #1, set $60.00 – $100.00.

Plate 182. Condiment set on round tray in blue and multicolored luster glazes, 5½" wide, tray and mustard Black Mark #52, pepper Black Mark #1, toothpick holder and salt no Mark, set $60.00 – $100.00.

Plate 183. Condiment set on deep tray in blue and multicolored luster glazes, pictured in the 1929 Sears & Roebuck Catalog with a different motif for $1.00, 3½" wide, all Black Mark #1, set $26.00 – $42.00.

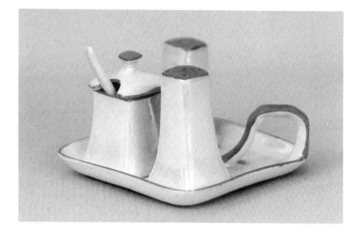

Plate 184. Noritake condiment set on square tray in white opalescent and orange luster glazes, tray 4" wide with no Mark, mustard Green Mark #53, salt and pepper Green Mark #1, set $30.00 - $55.00.

Plate 185. Condiment set on cloverleaf tray, 3¾" wide, all Black Mark #1, set $28.00 – $42.00.

Plate 186. Unusual condiment set in blue luster glaze with pepper shaker, built-in mustard pot, and salt dip (with salt in it to show it better), tray 4" wide with Red Mark #1, set $28.00 – $42.00.

Plate 187. Noritake condiment set on round tray in white and tan luster glazes with multicolored floral motif, 4¾" wide, tray and mustard Green Mark #53, salt and pepper Green Mark #1, set $45.00 – $65.00.

Plate 188. Noritake condiment set on long tray in tan luster with multicolored motif, 7½" wide, tray and mustard Green Mark #53, salt and pepper no Mark, set $65.00 – $95.00.

Plate 189. Condiment set on long tray in blue and black shiny glazes, 9" wide, tray and mustard Green Mark #10, salt and pepper no Mark, set $38.00 – $52.00.

Plate 190. Scenic condiment set on long tray in blue and yellow luster glazes with multicolored motif, 9½" wide, tray and mustard Red Mark #32, salt and pepper no Mark, set $38.00 – $52.00.

Plate 191. Bird condiment set on long tray in multicolored shiny and luster glazes, 7" wide, tray and mustard Black Mark #20, salt and pepper no Mark, set $45.00 – $65.00.

Plate 192. Bird condiment set on long tray in yellow luster glaze, 7¼" wide, all Red Mark #1, set $32.00 – $42.00.

Plate 193. Large duck condiment set on tray in multicolored luster glazes, 6¾" wide, tray Black Mark #1, other pieces no Mark, set $38.00 – $75.00.

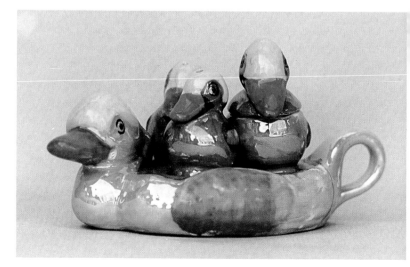

Plate 194. Elephant condiment set in tan luster glaze, 3¾", all Red Mark #1, set $20.00 – $35.00.

Plate 195. Goldcastle lotus blossom condiment set with frog finial in cream and tan luster glazes, 5½" wide, tray and mustard Black Mark #43, salt and pepper Black Mark #3, set $25.00 – $45.00.

Plate 196. (A) Flower basket condiment set on tray in teal and multicolored luster glazes, 4" wide, all Black Mark #1, set $30.00 – $45.00. (B) Goldcastle condiment set on tray in ivory luster glaze with multicolored floral motif, 4" wide, base Red Mark #43, salt and pepper Red Mark #3, mustard no Mark, set $25.00 – $40.00.

Plate 197. Boat condiment set in blue luster with multicolored motif, pictured in a pre-World War II Butler Bros. Catalog with a different motif for $.65 wholesale/$1.00 – $1.50 retail, 6½" wide, all Red Mark #1, base also Blind Mark #1, set $25.00 – $35.00.

Plate 198. Beer barrel condiment set on tray in multicolored shiny glazes, a post-World War II piece (the same figure was also made as a liquor set with barrel shot glasses), 5¾", tray Black Mark #1, other pieces no Mark, set $18.00 – $25.00.

In addition to the matching ceramic trays, figural salt and pepper sets were also sold on trays or holders of antimony (metal).

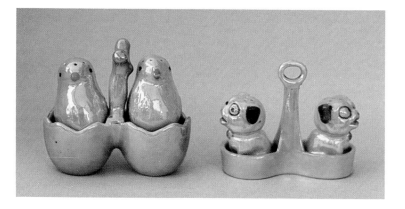

Plate 199. (A) Bird salt and pepper on swan tray in tan luster glaze (same birds as page 88), 5½" wide, tray Red Mark #25, salt and pepper Black Mark #1, set $20.00 – $35.00. (B) Bird salt and pepper on swan tray, 4" wide, tray Black Mark #25, salt and pepper Black Mark #1, set $20.00 – $35.00.

Plate 200. (A) Chick salt and pepper on tray in tan and blue luster glazes, 3½" wide, tray Green Mark #1, salt and pepper no Mark, set $20.00 – $35.00. (B) Dog salt and pepper on tray in tan luster glaze (the same tray was sold with other animal shakers, including birds), 3¼" wide, tray Red Mark #1, salt and pepper no Mark, set $18.00 – $28.00.

Plate 201. Rabbit salt and pepper on tray in multi-colored semi-matte glazes, 5¼" wide, tray Red Mark #25, salt and pepper Red Mark #1, set $25.00 – $35.00.

Plate 202. Frog on lily pad salt and pepper in multicolored shiny glazes, 4¼" wide, pad and frog Red Mark #2, lotus bud Red Mark #1, set $15.00 – $25.00.

Plate 203. (A) Camel salt and pepper in multicolored shiny glazes, 3", all Red Mark #1, set $18.00 – $22.00. (B) Dog salt and pepper in multicolored shiny glazes, 2½", base Black Mark #2, set $18.00 – $25.00.

Plate 204. (A) Fruit basket salt and pepper in green and multicolored matte glazes, 3½", base Brown Mark #1, salt and pepper no Mark, set $18.00 – $22.00. (B) Fruit basket salt and pepper in green and multicolored matte glazes, 3½", base Black Mark #1, salt and pepper no Mark, set $18.00 – $22.00.

Plate 205. Rare Japanese lady with lotus blossom salt and pepper on tray in multicolored luster and shiny glazes, 4" wide, Black Mark #1, set $25.00 – $50.00.

Plate 206. (A) Bellhop salt and pepper in multicolored shiny glazes, 3¾", Black Mark #2, set $40.00 – $65.00. (B) Hatbox lady salt and pepper in multicolored shiny glazes, 5¼", lady Black Mark #1, salt and pepper no Mark, set $40.00 – $65.00.

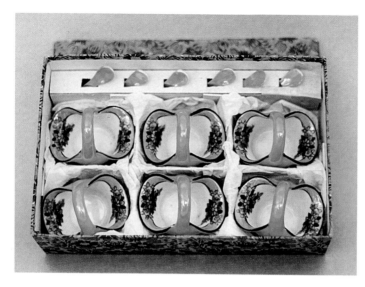

Plate 207. Noritake salt dip set in amber luster glaze with original box, all 1¾", all Red Mark #53, set $75.00 – $125.00.

Plate 208. Noritake salt dips in blue luster with multicolored figure, 1¾" wide, Green Mark #53, $25.00 – $45.00 each.

Plate 209. Double open salt in green and amber luster glazes with bluebird finial, 3¼", Red Mark #1, $25.00 – $40.00.

⚜ Cream and Sugar Sets ⚜

There are a lot more pitcher collectors than there are sugar bowl collectors, so by rights there should be more lone sugar bowls around, but that's not the case. Sugar bowls got harder use than cream pitchers, so there seem to be more lone creamers.

Plate 210. Orange cream and sugar on tray with multicolored enameling, 7½" wide, all Black Mark #1, set $32.00 – $42.00.

Plate 211. Tray with cream and sugar with shi shi finial in multicolored semi-matte glazes, 6½" wide, all Black Mark #56, set $35.00 – $45.00.

Plate 212. Elephant cream and sugar in multicolored luster glazes, pictured in the 1929 Sears & Roebuck Catalog for $1.00, 4¼", Red Mark #25, set $42.00 – $65.00.

Plate 213. Elephant cream and sugar with Asian figures in multicolored luster glazes, 5", Red Mark #25, set $42.00 – $65.00.

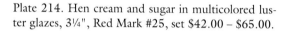
Plate 214. Hen cream and sugar in multicolored luster glazes, 3¼", Red Mark #25, set $42.00 – $65.00.

Plate 215. Duck cream and sugar in multicolored luster glazes, pictured in a pre-World War II Butler Bros. Catalog for $.65 wholesale/$1.00 – $1.50 retail, 3¼", Red Mark #25, set $42.00 – $65.00.

Plate 216. Cream and sugar in ivory and multicolored luster glazes, 4¾", Black Mark #1, set $22.00 – $36.00.

✎ Divided Relish Dishes ✎

These were also sold under many different names, including "relish dishes," "compartment relish dishes," "relish and celery dishes" (if one compartment was longer), and "divided relishes."

Plate 217. Covered divided relish in white shiny glaze with multicolored floral motif and reed handle, 11½" wide, Red Mark #1, $40.00 – $70.00.

Plate 218. Divided relish that looks like Italian ceramics in cream and multicolored matte glazes with pear handle, 9½" wide, Black Mark #1, $20.00 – $35.00.

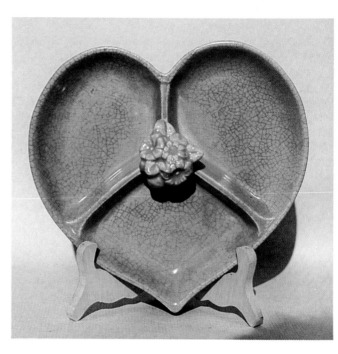

Plate 219. Heart-shaped divided relish in green crackle glaze, 7½", Black Mark #84, $15.00 – $25.00.

Plate 220. Club-shaped divided relish in green shiny glaze, 8", Black Mark #1, $15.00 – $25.00.

⚜ Egg Cups ⚜

Often the figural egg cups are more decorative than practical because they are hollow, so the yoke would run down into the foot of the piece if one actually tried to eat from it.

Plate 221. (A) Duck egg cup in multicolored shiny glazes, 3", Red Mark #1, $18.00 – $26.00. (B) Chick egg cup in yellow luster glaze, 2¾", Black Mark #1, $16.00 – $25.00.

Plate 222. (A) Duck egg cup in white and multicolored shiny glazes, 2", Red Mark #2, $8.00 – $15.00. (B) Pelican egg cup in white and multicolored shiny glazes, 2", Red Mark #2, $8.00 – $15.00.

Plate 223. (A) Bunny egg cup in tan luster and multicolored shiny glazes, 3¼", Black Mark #1, $16.00 – $26.00. (B) Chicken egg cup in multicolored luster and matte glazes, 2½", Black Mark #1, $16.00 – $26.00.

Plate 224. (A) Noritake scenic mountain egg cup in tan luster and multicolored shiny glazes, 3", Red Mark #26, $11.00 – $18.00. (B) Chicken egg cup in tan and yellow luster glazes, 2½", Red Mark #4, $16.00 – $23.00.

⚜ Egg Timers ⚜

To hold their value, egg timers must have the little glass timer bulb intact.

Plate 225. Bellhop egg timer in green and multicolored shiny glazes, 2¾", Black Mark #1 and Blind Mark #1, $24.00 – $35.00.

Plate 226. (A) Tall Dutch girl egg timer in orange and multicolored shiny glazes, 4", Black Mark #1, $24.00 – $35.00. (B) Girl egg timer in tan luster with multicolored shiny and matte glazes, 3½", Red Mark #2, $24.00 – $35.00. (C) Small Dutch girl egg timer in multicolored matte and shiny glazes, 2½", Black Mark #1, $20.00 – $30.00.

Plate 227. (A) Colonial lady egg timer in multicolored shiny glazes, 4¾", Black Mark #1 and Blind Mark #1, $24.00 – $35.00. (B) Calico rabbit egg timer, 3¼", Black Mark #2, $24.00 – $35.00. (C) Chef egg timer in blue and multicolored shiny glazes, 3¾", Black Mark #3, $24.00 – $35.00.

Plate 228. Veggie man egg timer in multicolored semi-matte glazes, 4", Black Mark #1, $24.00 – $35.00.

❧ Figurines ❧

The Japanese producers refer to human figurines as dolls, and the rest as novelties.

Plate 229. Bisque wedding party in original box, 3½" – 3¾" tall, all Blind Mark #1, box Marked "Made in Japan," $75.00 – $100.00.

Plate 230. Set of bisque quints (not the Dionnes because second from left is a boy) in original box, all 2¾", all Blind Mark #2, box Marked "Made in Japan," $75.00 – $150.00.

Plate 231. Rare World's Fair doll in purple and multicolored matte glazes, inscribed "San Francisco Fair 1939, 4", Red Mark #1, $25.00 – $50.00.

Plate 232. Rare bisque couple on swing with original cord tying them in, 5½", Black Mark #1 on wooden base, $35.00 – $60.00.

Plate 233. Skirtholder lady in orange and yellow shiny glazes, 6¾", Red Mark #30, $38.00 – $55.00.

Plate 234. Maruyama lady in multicolored semi-matte glazes, 6½", Red Mark #65, $18.00 – $28.00.

Plate 235. Boy in green and multicolored matte glazes, 8¼", $18.00 – $28.00.

Plate 237. Baby and bunny in multicolored shiny glazes, 2", Red Mark #51A, $12.00 – $22.00.

Plate 236. Rabbi in pulpit in black and white shiny glazes, probably part of a wedding set, 3½", Black Mark #2, $5.00 – $8.00.

Plate 238. Musician trio in multicolored matte glazes, 4¾", all Red Mark #1, set $25.00 – $38.00.

Plate 239. (A) Maruyama Hunt scene in multicolored shiny glazes, 4¼" wide, Red Mark #65 $45.00 – $65.00. (B) Standing rider in tan luster and multicolored shiny glazes, 3¼" wide, Red Mark #1 and Blind Mark #2 $35.00 – $52.00.

Plate 240. Goldcastle hunt scene in multicolored shiny glazes, 6" wide, Blue Mark #43A, $45.00 – $65.00.

Plate 241. Hitchhiking birds (the owner calls them Clark and Claudette) in multicolored shiny glazes, 3¼", (A) Black Mark #16, (B) no Mark, $15.00 – $25.00 each.

Plate 242. Scotties in multicolored shiny glazes. (A) 2¾", Red Mark #2, $10.00 – $20.00. (B) 3½", Black Mark #25, $12.00 – $22.00.

Plate 243. Large Scottie dog in multicolored shiny glazes, 10", Black Mark #2 and Blind Stamped with numbers "H227A63," $35.00 – $55.00.

Plate 244. Dog in green and maroon shiny glazes, 5¼", Black Mark #1, $18.00 – $28.00.

Plate 245. Dog in multicolored shiny glazes, as pictured in the 1931 Sears & Roebuck Catalog for $.49, 4½", Red Mark #25, $15.00 – $25.00.

Plate 246. (A) Scottie in multicolored shiny glazes, 4½", Black Mark #1, $12.00 – $22.00. (B) Elephant in multicolored shiny glazes, 4", Black Mark #23A, $8.00 – $15.00. (C) Cat in multicolored shiny glazes, 3½", Blue Mark #2, $8.00 – $15.00.

Plate 247. Three animals in white and multicolored shiny glazes. (A) Dog, 3¾", Red Mark #2, $12.00 – $22.00. (B) Pig, 3", Red Mark #2, $8.00 – $15.00. (C) Rabbit, 4¼", Black Mark #2, $15.00 – $25.00.

Plate 248. Cat and kitten in multicolored shiny glazes, 3½", Black Mark #1 and Blind Mark #1, $8.00 – $18.00.

Plate 249. Bunnies in multicolored luster glazes, 3¾" wide, Black Mark #1 and Blind Mark #2, $15.00 – $25.00.

Plate 250. Monkey in green shiny glaze, similar to German figurines, 5", Black Mark #1, $20.00 – $30.00.

Plate 251. Ram's head in cream matte glaze, 7¼", Blue Mark #1, $25.00 – $45.00.

Plate 252. Monkey orchestra in multicolored shiny glazes with gold luster trim, tallest 2", all Black Mark #1, except far left one has no Mark, $8.00 – $12.00 each.

Plate 253. Duck in multicolored shiny glazes, similar to older Chinese figurines but shown in the 1965 – 66 Norcrest Catalog on page 240 of this book, 6½", Black Mark #2 with original price $.89, $20.00 – $45.00.

Plate 254. Pheasant in multicolored shiny glazes, 6", Blind Mark #1, $25.00 – $45.00.

Plate 255. Ducks in multicolored shiny glazes, 4½", Blue Mark #23A, $20.00 – $40.00.

⚜ Fish Bowl Ornaments ⚜

Quality of glaze is very important in this category, because so often the pieces were used in the water. If the glaze has eroded away, the piece is severely devalued.

Plate 256. Mermaid on snail in multicolored matte glazes, 4", Red Mark #2, $32.00 – $55.00.

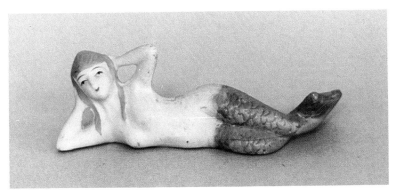

Plate 257. Bisque mermaid, 4¾" wide, Black Mark #2, $25.00 – 45.00.

Plate 258. Mermaid in multicolored matte glazes, 3½", Black Mark #2, $5.00 – $10.00 as shown.

Plate 259. Boy on dolphin in multicolored matte glazes, 3¾", Black Mark #38 and Blind Mark #1, $18.00 – $28.00.

Plate 260. (A) Diver in orange matte glaze, 3¼", Black Mark #2, $12.00 – $22.00. (B) Diver in white shiny glaze, 4¾", Black Mark #2, $12.00 – $22.00.

Plate 261. (A) Fish in multicolored matte and shiny glazes, 2½", Black Mark #40, $12.00 – $22.00. (B) Fish in multicolored shiny glazes, 3¼", Black Mark #2, $12.00 – $22.00.

Plate 262. (A) Castle in multicolored matte glazes, 2½", Black Mark #2, $15.00 – $20.00. (B) Castle in multicolored shiny glazes, 3", Black Mark #2, $2.00 – $4.00 as shown. (C) Castle in multicolored matte glazes, 2¼", Black Mark #2, $15.00 – $20.00.

Plate 263. (A) Castle in multicolored matte glazes, 3¾", Black Mark #2, $15.00 – $20.00. (B) Castle in multicolored shiny glazes, 4½", no Mark, $15.00 – $20.00.

Plate 264. Pagoda fish bowl ornaments in multicolored shiny glazes. (A) 3½", Black Mark #2, $15.00 – $20.00. (B) 3¼", Red Mark #2, $15.00 – $20.00

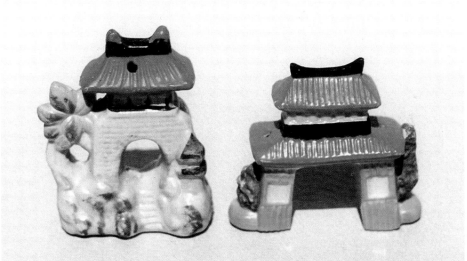

Plate 265. (A) Torii Gate in multicolored shiny glazes, 3¾", Black Mark #2, $15.00 – $20.00. (B) Castle in multicolored shiny glazes, 4¼", Black Mark #1, $15.00 – $20.00.

Plate 266. (A) Castle in multicolored matte glazes, 4", Black Mark #1, $15.00 – $20.00. (B) Castle in multicolored matte glazes, 3½", Red Mark #2, $15.00 – $20.00.

Plate 267. Fish bowl ornament in multicolored shiny glazes, 5", Red Mark #1, $5.00 – $10.00 as shown.

⩗ Flower Frogs ⩗

These were called "flower frogs," "flower blocks," "figural flower blocks," and "flower holders."

Plate 268. Circle of swans flower bowl with swan flower frog in multicolored luster glazes; bowl, 7" wide, Black Mark #1; frog, 5" tall, Black Mark #1; $75.00 – $125.00.

Plate 269. (A) Bird flower frog in blue and multicolored luster glazes, 5¼", Black Mark #1, $18.00 – $28.00. (B) Bird flower frog in bronze and multicolored luster glazes, 4½", Red Mark #66A, $18.00 – $28.00.

Plate 270. (A) Duck flower frog in amber and multicolored luster glazes, pictured in a pre-World War II Larkin Catalog for $1.00, 5", Black Mark #1, $18.00 – $28.00. (B) Bird flower frog in multicolored luster glazes, 4¾", Red Mark #74, $18.00 – $28.00.

Plate 271. (A) Bird flower frog in blue luster and red shiny glazes, 5¼", Black Mark #1, $18.00 – $28.00. (B) Bird flower frog in tan and blue luster glaze, 6", Black Mark #52, $18.00 – $28.00.

Plate 272. Bird flower frog with ivy and red berries in tan and multicolored luster glazes, 5¾", Black Mark #2, $18.00 – $28.00.

Plate 273. (A) Bird flower frog in multicolored shiny glazes, 6½", Blind Mark #85, $15.00 – $22.00. (B) Bird flower frog in multicolored matte glazes, 6", Blind Mark #1, $15.00 – $22.00.

Plate 274. (A) Small bird flower frog in multicolored luster glazes, 2¾", Red Mark #1, $12.00 – $22.00. (B) Small bird flower frog in tan luster with multicolored matte and shiny glazes, 3¼", Red Mark #1, $12.00 – $22.00.

Plate 275. Floral bud flower frog in multicolored luster and shiny glazes, 2½", Black Mark #1, $12.00 – $22.00.

Plate 276. Rosebud flower frog in multicolored luster glazes, 2½", Red Mark #1, $12.00 – $22.00.

Plate 277. Lotus bud flower frog in multicolored shiny glazes, 4½" wide, Black Mark #1, $12.00 – $18.00.

⚔ Incense Burners ⚔

Not only was burning incense a popular method of masking the odor of cigarette smoke, the burners themselves were a popular accessory in the 1920s and 1930s. They were promoted heavily in catalogs and ads of the day, and they often came boxed with incense cones. There was a lot of interest in Oriental and Egyptian novelties, and incense burners added that exotic touch. Incense burners experienced a revival in the late 1960s and 1970s, but these were usually more modern looking.

Plate 278. Incense burner set in original box, a pre-World War II piece from the Akiyama Store, burner and tray are metal, cone incense is in the box with a newspaper scrap referring to the Japanese governing of China, box is 3½" wide, $15.00 – $25.00.

Plate 279. Man on elephant incense burner in multicolored luster glazes, 6¼", Red Mark #74, $25.00 – $55.00.

Plate 280. (A) Egyptian girl incense burner in tan luster and multicolored shiny glazes, 5½", Blind Mark #1, $50.00 – $75.00. (B) Flower girl in tan luster with multicolored shiny glazes, 5½", Red Mark #1, $50.00 – $75.00.

Plate 281. Buddha incense burner in tan luster glaze, 4¼", Black Mark #1, $20.00 – $30.00.

Plate 282. (A) Bisque incense burner inscribed "KIBITZER," 3", Black Mark #2, $20.00 – $30.00. (B) Chalk incense burner in multicolored matte glazes, 5¼", Blind Mark #1, $15.00 – $22.00.

Plate 283. (A) Mini Oriental incense burner, 2½", no Mark, $3.00 – $8.00. (B) Figural incense burner in blue and multi-colored shiny glazes, 3¾", Blind Mark partly obscured, possibly #1 or #72, $15.00 – $25.00.

Plate 284. Seated gent incense burner in multicolored shiny glazes, 4¼", Black Mark #2, $20.00 – $30.00.

Plate 285. Elephant and pagoda incense
burner in multicolored shiny glazes, 5¾",
Red Mark #1, $15.00 – $25.00.

Plate 286. Pagoda two-piece incense
burner in blue and tan luster glazes, 6¼",
Black Mark #1, $15.00 – $25.00.

Plate 287. Incense burner in orange and black shiny glazes, 3¼", no
Mark, $12.00 – $22.00.

Plate 288. (A) Incense burner in tan and blue luster
glazes, 3¼", no Mark, $12.00 – $22.00. (B) Floral
incense burner in multicolored matte glazes, 2¾",
Blind Mark #1, $12.00 – $22.00.

The pieces on the next two pages were originally a boxed set; unfortunately, the dealer did not save the carton. All are earthenware in multicolored shiny glazes, and the ones without the coin slots are similar to the assorted styles of incense burners featured in the Sears & Roebuck Catalogs of 1929.

Plate 289. (A) Ship inscribed "INCENSE BURNER BANK" with coin slot on top of sail and incense cavity in rear, 4½", Black Mark #1. (B) Grampus (the symbol of Nagoya Castle in Japan) inscribed "INCENSE BURNER BANK" with coin slot in mouth and cavity in rear, 4½" Black Mark #1. $12.00 – $22.00 each.

Plate 290. (A) Indian temple incense burner, 4½", Blind Mark #1. (B) Pagoda inscribed "INCENSE BURNER BANK" with coin slot on front and cavity in rear, 4½", Black Mark #1. $12.00 – $22.00 each.

Plate 291. (A) Torii Gate incense burner, 4", Blind Mark #1. (B) Pagoda incense burner, 4¾", Blind Mark #1. $12.00 – $22.00 each.

Plate 292. (A) Lighthouse incense burner, 5½", Blind Mark #2. (B) Domed house incense burner, 3½", Blind Mark #1. $12.00 – $22.00 each.

Plate 293. (A) Cottage incense burner, 4½", Blind Mark #1. (B) Cottage incense burner, 4¼", Blind Mark #1. $12.00 – $22.00 each.

Plate 294. These two pieces came with the boxed set in plates 289 – 293: (A) Sailboat (has smoke hole in back; perhaps it originally came with a base), 4½", Blind Mark #1 and Red Mark #38, $8.00 – $15.00. (B) Sailing ship (no smoke hole), 4¼", Black Mark #1, $8.00 – $15.00.

⚜ Kitchenware ⚜

To begin with, here is a grouping of Moriyama ware, a distinctive and highly collectible line of kitchenware in cream, green, and black shiny glazes.

Plate 295. Moriyama ware nesting bowls, 8¼", 7", and 5¾", Black Mark #30A, set $50.00 – $65.00.

Plate 296. Moriyama ware cake plate, pictured in the 1935 Sears & Roebuck Catalog as "Taisho Ware" for $.59, 12¼", Black Mark #1, $20.00 – $45.00. Cake server, 10½", Black Mark #30, $25.00 – $50.00.

Plate 297. Moriyama ware cheese dish, 6¼" long, Black Mark #30, $30.00 – $40.00.

Plate 298. (A) and (C)
Moriyama ware cream
4¼" and sugar 5", Black
Mark #30, set $25.00 –
$55.00. (B) Moriyama
ware drippings jar, 5",
Black Mark #30A,
$25.00 – $45.00.

Plate 299. (A) Moriyama ware cup
and saucer, Black Mark #30,
$15.00 – $25.00. (B) Teapot, 6½",
Black Mark #30, $25.00 – $55.00.

Plate 300. Moriyama ware covered dish, 9½" wide, Black Mark
#30, $25.00 – $55.00.

Plate 301. Moriyama ware oval covered refrigerator dish, 6",
Black Mark #30, $23.00 – $34.00.

Plate 302. (A) and (C) Moriyama ware salt and pepper, 5", Black Mark #30, $20.00 – $35.00. (B) Moriyama ware salt box, 6½", Black Mark #1, $45.00 – $65.00.

Plate 303. Moriyama ware handled tray, 10¼" wide, Black Mark #30A, $30.00 – $45.00.

What we refer to today as biscuit barrels were sold as cookie jars or barrels, cracker jars or barrels, and biscuit barrels.

Plate 304. Goldcastle biscuit barrel in tan and multicolored luster glazes, 6", Red Mark #43, $45.00 – $65.00.

Plate 305. (A) Cactus biscuit barrel in green and multicolored shiny glazes, 7", Black Mark #1, $45.00 – $65.00. (B) Strawberry biscuit barrel in red and green shiny glazes, 7", Black Mark #1, $45.00 – $65.00.

Plate 306. (A) Windmill biscuit barrel in cream and multi-colored shiny glazes, 6½", Black Mark #1, $45.00 – $65.00. (B) House biscuit barrel in cream and multicolored shiny glazes, 6¾", Black Mark #1, $45.00 – $65.00.

Plate 307. (A) House biscuit barrel in green and multicolored shiny glazes, 8", Black Mark #1, $45.00 – $65.00. (B) Stippled biscuit barrel with floral motif in cream and multicolored shiny glazes, 6", Black Mark #1, $45.00 – $65.00.

Plate 308. (A) Biscuit barrel with cherries in white shiny glaze with multicolored motif, 6", Mark obscured, $45.00 – $65.00. (B) Basketweave biscuit barrel in cream shiny glaze with multicolored fruits, 5", Black Mark #1, $30.00 – $45.00.

Plate 309. (A) Biscuit barrel in blue and multicolored shiny glazes with floral motif, 5", Black Mark #86, $40.00 – $60.00. (B) Biscuit barrel in cream and multicolored shiny glazes with berry motif, 8½", $45.00 – $65.00.

Plate 310. (A) Biscuit barrel with raspberries in cream shiny glaze with multicolored motif, 6¾", Black Mark #1, $45.00 – $65.00. (B) Biscuit barrel in cream crackle glaze with multicolored tulips, 5", Black Mark #1, $45.00 – $65.00.

Plate 311. (A) Biscuit barrel in cream shiny glaze with multicolored floral motif, 7", Black Mark #1, $45.00 – $65.00. (B) Biscuit barrel in green shiny glaze with multicolored floral motif, 8", Black Mark #1, $45.00 – $65.00.

Plate 312. (A) Imitation Belleek biscuit barrel with green shamrocks on cream shiny glaze, 5¼", Black Mark #1, $45.00 – $65.00. (B) Biscuit barrel with green flowers on cream shiny glaze, 5½", Black Mark #29, $45.00 – $65.00.

Plate 313. (A) Biscuit barrel in lavender shiny glaze with multicolored floral motif, 8", Black Mark #1, $45.00 – $65.00. (B) Biscuit barrel in blue shiny glaze with multicolored fruit motif, 6½", Blind Mark #1, $45.00 – $65.00.

Plate 314. (A) Hunt scene biscuit barrel in black and cream shiny glazes, 5¾", no Mark, $45.00 – $65.00. (B) Biscuit barrel with Oriental ladies in cream and multicolored shiny glazes, 6", Black Mark #22, $45.00 – $65.00.

Plate 315. (A) Biscuit barrel in cream and yellow shiny glazes with multicolored floral motif, 7¾", Black Mark #87, $45.00 – $65.00. (B) Biscuit barrel in cream shiny glaze with multicolored floral motif, 6½", Blind Mark #1, $45.00 – $65.00.

Plate 316. (A) Dragon biscuit barrel in cream and multicolored crackle glazes, 5½", Black Mark #1, $45.00 – $65.00. (B) Pineapple biscuit barrel in cream and multicolored shiny glazes, 6", no Mark, $45.00 – $65.00.

Plate 317. (A) Shaped biscuit barrel with bird finial in maroon and cream shiny glazes with multicolored motif, 6½", Black Mark #1, $45.00 – $65.00. (B) Shaped biscuit barrel with cherubs in green shiny glaze, 6", Black Mark #1, $45.00 – $65.00.

Plate 318. (A) Biscuit barrel in cream shiny glaze with multicolored classical figures and flower finial, 8", Black Mark #2, $45.00 – $65.00. (B) Biscuit barrel in cream shiny glaze with multicolored musicians, 5", Black Mark #1, $40.00 – $60.00.

Plate 319. (A) Biscuit barrel with cherubs in blue and multicolored shiny glazes, 7", Blind Mark #1, $45.00 – $65.00. (B) Biscuit barrel with hunt scene motif in blue and cream shiny glazes, 8", Black Mark #1, $45.00 – $65.00.

Plate 320A. Small cannister set in cream crackle glaze with multicolored floral motif, 5½", Black Mark #28, $10.00 – $20.00 each.

Plate 320B. Tall cannister set in cream crackle glaze with multicolored floral motif, matching those in plate 320A, 9", Black Mark #28, $15.00 – $25.00 each.

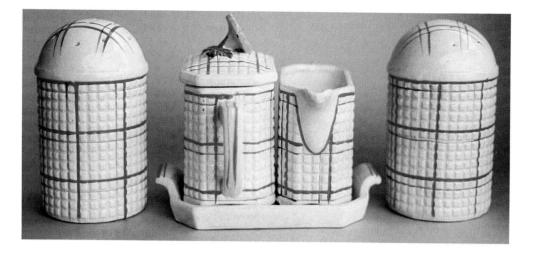

Plate 321. (A) and (C) Salt and pepper in cream crackle glaze with multicolored trim, 5½", Black Mark #1, set $20.00 – $35.00. (B) Cream and sugar on tray in multicolored crackle glaze with multicolored trim and yellow flower finial, 6½" wide, Black Mark #1, set $50.00 – $85.00.

Plate 322. (A) and (C) Cream, 3", and sugar, 4", in imitation Belleek glazes with multicolored butterfly finial, Green Mark #1, set $25.00 – $40.00. (B) Salt and pepper on tray in imitation Belleek glazes, 3¾" wide, salt and pepper Black Mark #2, tray Black Mark "OCCUPIED JAPAN," $15.00 – $25.00. (This type of ware was pictured in the 1970 Norcrest Catalog in Volume 1 of *The Collector's Guide to Made in Japan*.)

Plate 323. Basketweave cream and sugar in cream and multicolored shiny glazes, 4¾" tall, Black Mark #1, $20.00 – $35.00. (This type of ware was pictured in the 1970 Norcrest Catalog in Volume 1 of *The Collector's Guide to Made in Japan*.)

Plate 324. Rare Domino cream and sugar in cream shiny glaze with multicolored floral motif (named for the brand of sugar cubes that fit in the tray like little sugar rays), 10½" wide, no Mark, $25.00 – $55.00.

Plate 325. Shakers in green shiny glaze with multicolored floral motif, 5", Black Mark #29, $10.00 – $18.00 each.

Plate 326. Shaped shakers in cream crackle glaze with multicolored floral motif, 5¾", all Black Mark #1, $10.00 – $18.00 each.

Plate 327. (A) Single shaker in cream and green crackle glaze, 5", Black Mark #1, $10.00 – $18.00. (B) and (C) Pair of shakers, 5", Black Mark #24, $10.00 – $18.00 each.

Plate 328. (A) and (C) Salt and pepper in cream crackle glaze with multicolored floral motif, 4¾", Black Mark #28, $10.00 – $18.00 each. (B) Egg cup, 3¼", Black Mark #28, $11.00 – $18.00.

Plate 329. (A) and (C) Salt and pepper in cream shiny glaze with multicolored floral motif, 5¼", Black Mark #1, $10.00 – $18.00 each. (B) Cruet set on tray, 7½" wide, Black Mark #1, $25.00 – $40.00.

Plate 330. Pancake or waffle set in multicolored shiny glazes, Tray 10¾" wide, Black Mark #1, $35.00 – $55.00.

Plate 331. (A) Pitcher in cream shiny glaze with red cherries, 7", Black Mark #14 with no patent, $15.00 – $35.00. (B) Pitcher, 4", Black Mark #14 with no patent, $12.00 – $30.00. (C) Salt and pepper, 2½", Gold Mark #14 with patent number 77233, set $18.00 – $25.00.

Plate 332. Circle pitcher in multicolored shiny glazes, 9", Black Mark #1, $24.00 – $38.00.

Plate 333. Pitcher set in green and mult colored shiny glazes, 8½", Black Mar #73, $45.00 – $65.00.

Plate 334. German beer stein-type pitcher set, 8¾", Black Mark #1, $25.00 – $35.00 as pictured ($45.00 – $65.00 complete with four or six tumblers).

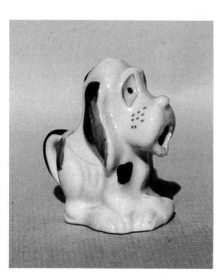

Plate 335. Dog pitcher in multicolored shiny glazes, 2¾", Black Mark #1, $22.00 – $30.00

Plate 336. Rooster pitcher in multicolored shiny glazes, 5", Blue Mark #2, $20.00 – $25.00.

Plate 337. Green shiny glazed pitcher with black cat handle, 6¾", Black Mark #1, $20.00 – $35.00.

Plate 338. (A) Clown reamer in multicolored shiny glazes, 6½", Black Mark #1, $65.00 – $75.00. (B) Lotus reamer in multicolored shiny and luster glazes, 5", Red Mark #1, $50.00 – $65.00.

Plate 339. (A) Reamer in cream shin[y] glaze with multicolored floral moti[f], 6", Black Mark #28, $50.00 – $65.0[0]. (B) Drippings jar, 2¾", Black Mar[k] #28, $18.00 – $25.00.

Plate 340. Cat spice set in black shiny glaze on brown clay body in wooden rack, 11½" overall, all Yellow Mark #2, $18.00 – $35.00.

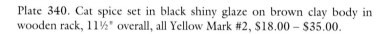

Plate 341. Bee honey pots in multicolored shiny glazes with origina[l] plastic spoons and original box, pots 2", both Black Mark #2, se[t] $20.00 – $30.00.

Plate 342. Ice box set in green and lavender shiny glazes, 6½" wide, bottom box only Black Mark #72, set $39.00 – $65.00.

Plate 343. Marmalade or jam pot in aqua and multicolored matte glazes, 4", Black Mark #1, $22.00 – $42.00.

Plate 344. Bonzo mustard in multicolored luster and shiny glazes, 3¾", Red Mark #1, $35.00 – $55.00.

Orange-Glazed Kitchenware

This type of kitchenware was very popular around World War II, and pieces are often found with the "Occupied Japan" Mark.

Plate 345. Cream and sugar on tray, 11" wide, cream and sugar Black Mark #14 with patent number 69429, tray Black Mark #50 with Japanese Patent No. 71952, set $25.00 – $40.00.

Plate 346. (A) Handled plate, 5¼", Black Mark #1, $8.00 – $12.00. (B) Salt and pepper on tray inscribed "Misquansut Beach NY," 5" wide, salt and pepper Black Mark #1, tray Black Mark #50, $18.00 – $28.00.

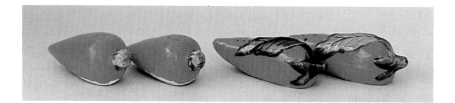

Plate 347. (A) Carrot salt and pepper, 2¼", Red Mark #2, $10.00 – $15.00. (B) Carrot salt and pepper, 3", Black Mark #2, $10.00 – $15.00.

Plate 348. Tomato salt and pepper, 2", Green Mark #2, $10.00 – $18.00.

⚑ Lamps ⚑

Electric lamps, especially boudoir lamps, have grown in popularity in recent years.

Plate 349. Pair of colonial lamps in white shiny glaze, 6¼", Black Mark #1, pair $30.00 – $55.00.

Plate 350. Pair of colonial lamps in white shiny and multicolored semi-matte glazes, pictured in the 1935 Sears & Roebuck Catalog at $1.00 for one lamp with a flowered shade and an "On and Off Snap Button," 7½", Black Mark #1, pair $45.00 – $75.00.

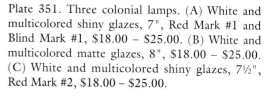

Plate 351. Three colonial lamps. (A) White and multicolored shiny glazes, 7", Red Mark #1 and Blind Mark #1, $18.00 – $25.00. (B) White and multicolored matte glazes, 8", $18.00 – $25.00. (C) White and multicolored shiny glazes, 7½", Red Mark #2, $18.00 – $25.00.

Plate 352. Colonial lamp in white shiny glaze, 8", Red Mark #1, $20.00 – $35.00.

Plate 353. Pierrot with lady lamp, 7", Black Mark #2, $20.00 – $35.00.

Plate 354. (A) Pierrot lamp with lady, 6¼", Black Mark #89, $20.00 – $35.00. (B) Pierrot lamp with lady, 6", Black Mark #89, $20.00 – $35.00.

Plate 355. Bird lamp in blue and multicolored luster glazes, 5½", Mark covered, $58.00 – $80.00.

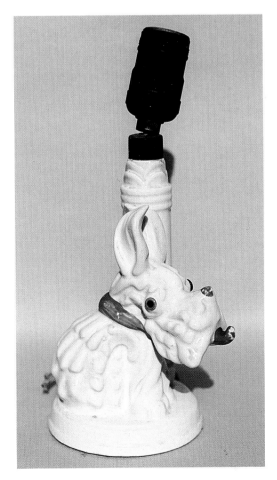

Plate 356. Scottie dog lamp in white shiny glaze with glass eyes, 6¾", Black Mark #25, $20.00 – $35.00.

Detail of owl lamp and base.

Plate 357. Two-piece owl lamp in blue and multicolored luster glazes, 5½", Black Mark #1, $50.00 – $75.00.

Plate 358. Chamberstick lamp in tan luster with multicolored floral motif (the candle is actually a light bulb), 5½" wide, Red Mark #25 with "NIPPON REGISTRATION GRANTED," $20.00 – $35.00.

Plate 359. (A) Oil lamp in white shiny glaze with rose decals, 8½", Black label with "JAPAN," $15.00 – $25.00. (B) Oil lamp in gray luster with moriage motif and Mt. Rushmore decal, 5½", Label #109, $15.00 – $25.00.

⚏ Lemon Servers ⚏

These were also sold as "candy," "mint," and "bonbon" dishes. If sold as "lemon," "pickle," or "olive" servers, they often came with a little, carved white bone fork. This type of dish is one of the most multiple of the multiple function items!

Plate 360. Two Noritake lemon servers, both Red Mark #53. (A) Orange and multicolored shiny glaze with bird motif, 6". (B) Checkerboard motif in multicolored shiny glazes, 5½". $25.00 – $50.00 each.

Plate 361. Lemon server with puffed-out motif in multicolored luster glazes, 6", Blue Mark #1, $25.00 – $45.00.

Plate 362. Noritake lemon servers, both 5¾" with Red Mark #53. (A) Cream semi-matte glaze with multicolored floral motif. (B) Blue luster and white shiny glaze with multicolored floral motif. $20.00 – $35.00 each.

Plate 363. (A) Noritake lemon server in blue luster with multicolored shiny glaze scene, 6¼", Green Mark #53, $20.00 – $35.00. (B) Noritake lemon server in tan luster glaze with multicolored fruit and floral motif, 5¾", Red Mark #53, $20.00 – $35.00.

Plate 364. Noritake scenic lemon server in multicolored matte glazes, 5¼", Red Mark #53, $20.00 – $35.00.

◁ Liquor Items ▷

The older liquor items have always been popular and pricey, but recently the newer pieces, such as plate #377, are showing up at shows and shops with higher price tags.

Plate 365. Multicolored bisque lady with umbrella and biting dog on brown shiny glazed flask inscribed "Just a Little Nip," 4½", Black Mark #1, $65.00 – $125.00.

Plate 366. Goldcastle flask in amber and gray luster glazes — look closely, the motif seems to be golfers playing croquet, inscribed "SOUVENIR OF ANAHEIM," metal lid is shot glass, 6", Black Mark #43, $85.00 – $110.00.

Plate 367. (A) Flask in multicolored luster and shiny glazes inscribed "ALL SCOTCH," 5¼", Black Mark #38, $40.00 – $65.00. (B) Decanter in multicolored luster and matte glazes inscribed "Farm Relief," 5½", Black Mark #1, $40.00 – $65.00. (C) Maruyama jug in multicolored shiny and matte glazes inscribed "NEVER DRINK WATER," 6½", Red Mark #65, $40.00 – $65.00.

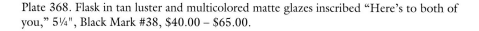

Plate 368. Flask in tan luster and multicolored matte glazes inscribed "Here's to both of you," 5¼", Black Mark #38, $40.00 – $65.00.

Plate 369. Rare bellhop liquor set in multicolored shiny glazes, 11", decanter Black Mark #1, shots no Mark, $100.00 – $155.00.

Plate 370. Decanter in tan luster with multicolored shiny glazes inscribed "Prohibition," 5", Black Mark #1, $50.00 – $75.00.

Plate 371. Camel decanter set in brown and multicolored semi-matte glazes, tray 6½" wide, Red Mark #25, $75.00 – $100.00 as pictured ($100.00 – $175.00 if complete with six shots).

Plate 372. Clown set in multicolored shiny glazes, 9", decanter Black Mark #1, shots no Mark, $50.00 – $75.00.

Plate 373. Scotsman set in brown and multicolored matte glazes on brown clay body, inscribed "Never drink Water Old Scotch," 9", decanter Label #110, shots no Mark, $20.00 – $40.00.

Plate 374. (A) Soldier set in multicolored shiny glazes, 11", Mark #81, set $25.00 – $45.00. (B) Red-eyed drunk set in multicolored shiny glazes, 11", paper label #112, set $25.00 – $45.00.

Plate 375. Cowboy decanter in multicolored shiny glazes, 8½", Black Mark #2, $20.00 – $35.00.

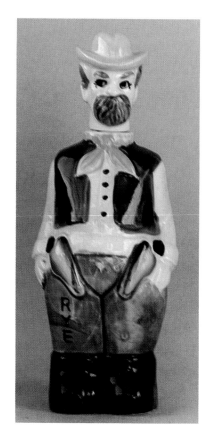

Plate 376. Decanter in purple and multicolored shiny glazes, 8½", Black Mark #1, $20.00 – $35.00.

Plate 377. Jug with naughty nude stopper in multicolored shiny glazes inscribed "LAY OFF THE OLD MAN'S PRIVATE STUFF," 8¾", Black Mark #2, $15.00 – $25.00.

Plate 378. (A) Gentleman decanter in multicolored shiny glazes, 9½", Black Mark #2, $20.00 – $35.00. (B) Soda jerk decanter in multicolored shiny glazes, 10½", marked "BOTTLE MADE IN JAPAN," $50.00 – $75.00. (C) Waiter decanter in multicolored shiny glazes, 9½", Black Mark #2, $20.00 – $35.00.

Plate 379. (A) Drunken-eyed decanter in multicolored shiny glazes, 8¼", Black Mark #1, $20.00 – $35.00. (B) Clown decanter in multicolored shiny glazes, 8¾", Black Mark #2, $20.00 – $35.00.

⚜ Match Holders ⚜

It's sometimes hard to tell a toothpick from a match holder, so it's in the eye of the beholder!

Plate 380. Bisque skeleton match holder with movable legs, 3", Black Mark #1 $65.00 – $85.00.

Plate 381. (A) Naughty bisque match holder inscribed "WHAT A BUST, VANCOUVER, WASH," 3¾", Red Mark #1, $25.00 – $35.00. (B) Naughty bisque match holder inscribed "ON THE BUST," 4½", Black Mark #2, $25.00 – $35.00.

Plate 382. Winking man cigarette or match holder in multicolored luster and shiny glazes, 5", Red Mark #1, $25.00 – $35.00.

Plate 383. (A) Oriental figure match holder in multicolored luster and shiny glazes, 5", Black Mark #1, $15.00 – $28.00. (B) Oriental figure ashtray in multicolored luster and shiny glazes, 5¼", Black Mark #1, $15.00 – $28.00.

Plate 384. Match holder with striker grooves in multicolored matte glazes, 2¼", Red Mark #1, $20.00 – $30.00.

⚞ Mayonnaise Sets ⚟

Some 1920s ads refer to the ball-footed bowl sets as "whipped cream sets" and the flat-bottomed bowl sets as "mayonnaise sets", while others refer to either style as "whipped cream or mayonnaise sets." The common usage today seems to be mayonnaise sets. Also, the sets were sold more commonly with liner plates, but I have seen at least one old ad showing the bowl and spoon alone as a set.

Plate 385. Opposites attract! Two Meito mirror image mayonnaise sets in blue and tan luster glazes, plates 5½", both Red and Green Mark #64, $15.00 – $25.00 per set.

Plate 386. Mayonnaise sets in multicolored luster glazes, plates 6½" wide, pictured in the 1929 Sears & Roebuck Catalog for $1.00 per set. (A) Ladle and bowl Red Mark #1, plate no Mark, $32.00 – $52.00. (B) Noritake, ladle and bowl, Blue Mark #26, plate no Mark, $35.00 – $65.00.

Plate 387. Goldcastle mayonnaise set in white luster glaze with multicolored enameling, plate 6½" wide with Black Mark #43, $32.00 – $52.00.

Plate 388. (A) Mayonnaise set with multicolored tree motif and tan luster interior, plate 6½" wide, bowl and plate Red Mark #21A, $32.00 – $52.00. (B) Amber and aqua luster mayonnaise set, plate 6½" wide, plate and bowl Black Mark #52, $32.00 – $52.00.

Plate 389. Mayonnaise set in multicolored luster glazes, plate 6" wide, bowl and plate Black Mark #1, $32.00 – $52.00.

Plate 390. Mayonnaise set in multicolored luster glazes with bird motif, plate 6" wide, plate and bowl Black Mark #1, $32.00 – $52.00.

Plate 391. Mayonnaise set in blue and multicolored luster glazes with sceni[c] motif (a pre-World War II piece from the Akiyama store), plate 6" wide, bowl and plate Black Mark #1, $32.00 – $52.00.

Plate 392. Meito mayonnaise set in multicolored shiny glazes with scenic motif, plate 5½", Green Mark #64, $25.00 – $45.00.

Plate 393. Mayonnaise set in blue and tan luster glazes with multicolored bird motif, plate 6¼", plate and bowl Black Mark #1, $32.00 – $52.00.

Plate 394. Mayonnaise set in orange shiny glaze with white cherry blossom motif, plate 6" wide, Blue Mark #52, $25.00 – $45.00.

⊿ Nut Cups ⊾

Collectors can be passionate about definitions — depending on what area you are collecting in, you might prefer to call these items match holders, salts or ring baskets. Since objects were often advertised with multiple uses, or simply offered for sale with no label or sign for intended use, we will refer to them as nut cups.

Plate 395. (A) Duck nut cup in multicolored shiny glazes, 1¾", Red Mark #2, $15.00 – $25.00. (B) Bunny nut cup in multicolored shiny glazes, 1¾", Red Mark #2, $15.00 – $25.00.

Plate 396. (A) Nut cup in yellow luster with blue forget-me-nots, 2", Black Mark #1, $16.00 – $23.00. (B) Nut cup in blue luster with multicolored floral motif, 3¼", Red Mark #1, $16.00 – $23.00.

Plate 397. Pair of Oriental figurine nut cups in multicolored matte glazes, 3", Red Mark #1, $16.00 – $22.00 each.

Plate 398. (A) and (C) Dog nut cups in tan luster and multicolored shiny glazes, 2", Black Mark #2, $16.00 – $22.00 each. (B) Girl and basket nut cup in multicolored shiny glazes, 3¼", Black Mark #2, $13.00 – $19.00.

Plate 399. (A) Dog nut cup in multicolored shiny glazes, 2", Black Mark #2. (B) Dutch boy nut cup in multicolored shiny glazes, 2¾", Black Mark #1. (C) Monkey nut cup in multicolored shiny glazes, 2", Black Mark #2. $16.00 – $22.00 each.

Plate 400. Man with banjo nut cup in multicolored shiny glazes, 2½", Black Mark #1, $16.00 – $22.00.

Plate 401. Geisha Girl nut cups in red and multicolored shiny glazes, 3" wide, no Mark, $10.00 – $20.00 each.

⚞ Pincushions ⚟

Pincushions are another multiple use item, and it can be hard for collectors to decide whether they are pincushions or cache pots, especially since their original owners often rooted plants in them.

Plate 402. Boxed Hans and Gretchen pincushion set in multicolored luster and shiny glazes. (Wrapped in Japanese newspaper referring to the invasion of Manchuria in 1931, these were pictured in the 1932 Sears & Roebuck Catalog for $.19 per pair.) Both Black Mark #1 and Blind Mark #1, box stamped "5045 Made in Japan," boxed set $50.00 – $95.00.

Plate 403. (A) Maruyama-style lady with duck pincushion in multicolored shiny glazes, 4¼", Red Mark #1 (although she is not marked with #65, I saw this piece at the factory in Japan), $18.00 – $25.00. (B) Lady pincushion in multicolored shiny glazes, 5", Red Mark #2, $15.00 – $25.00. (C) Dutch girl pincushion in multicolored luster and matte glazes, 3¾", Black Mark #1, $15.00 – $25.00.

Plate 404. (A) Santa driving a coach pincushion in multicolored luster and matte glazes, 3", Black Mark #38, $15.00 – $25.00. (B) Hummel-style girl pincushion in multicolored shiny glazes, 3", Black Mark #1, $15.00 – $25.00. (C) Dutch boy pincushion in multicolored luster and shiny glazes, 3¼", Black Mark #1 and Blind Mark #2, $12.00 – $18.00.

Plate 405. (A) Girl with basket pincushion in multicolored luster and shiny glazes, inscribed "From Frank Pattee Xmas 1931," 5", Black Mark #1, $20.00 – $32.00. (B) Two boys pincushion in multicolored luster and shiny glazes, 4", Black Mark #2, $20.00 – $32.00. (C) Pixie pincushion in multicolored luster and shiny glazes, 3½", Black Mark #1, $20.00 – $32.00.

Plate 406. Maruyama pincushions in multicolored luster glazes, 3", Red Mark #65 and Blind Mark #1, $20.00 – $32.00 each.

Plate 407. (A) Kewpie-style pincushion in multicolored shiny glazes, 4", Black Mark #1 and Blind Mark #1, $28.00 – $38.00. (B) Lady pincushion in multicolored shiny glazes, 3¾", Black Mark #1 and Blind Mark #1, $20.00 – $32.00.

Plate 408. (A) Bisque boy pincushion, 3", Blind Mark #1, $23.00 – $33.00. (B) Bisque boy pincushion, 2¾", Blind Mark #1, $20.00 – $30.00.

Plate 409. (A) Bisque girl pincushion, 3¼", Black Mark #1 and Blind Mark #1, $23.00 – $33.00. (B) Bisque girl pincushion, 3½", Blind Mark #1, $23.00 – $33.00.

Plate 410. (A) Girl pincushion in multicolored luster and shiny glazes, 3¼", Black Mark #1 and Blind Mark #1, $28.00 – $38.00. (B) Girl pincushion in multicolored luster and shiny glazes, 3½", Red Mark #1 and Blind Mark #1, $20.00 – $32.00.

Plate 411. (A) Dog pincushion in multicolored shiny glazes, 2¾", Black Mark #1, $13.00 – $22.00. (B) Clown pincushion in multicolored luster and matte glazes, 4", Black Mark #1, $19.00 – $23.00.

Plate 412. (A) Blue luster dog pincushion, 3¼", Blue Mark #1, $18.00 – $27.00. (B) Tan luster camel pincushion, 4", Black Mark #1, $28.00 – $38.00.

Plate 413. (A) Dog pincushion in multicolored shiny glazes, 4¼", Red Mark #1, $13.00 – $22.00. (B) Maruyama pincushion in multicolored shiny glazes, 2¾", Red Mark #65, $13.00 – $22.00.

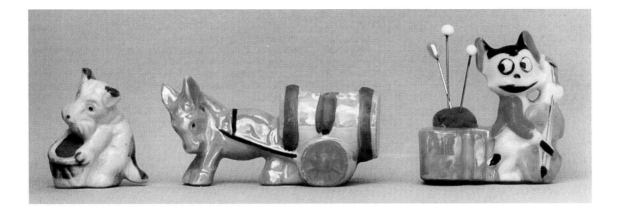

Plate 414. (A) Scottie pincushion in multicolored shiny glazes, 1¾", Blind Mark #1, $12.00 – $20.00. (B) Donkey pincushion in multicolored luster and shiny glazes, 1½", Black Mark #2, $12.00 – $20.00. (C) Card suit cat pincushion (cushion holder is club-shaped) in multicolored luster and shiny glazes, 2½", Black Mark #1, $13.00 – $22.00.

Plate 415. (A) Rabbit pincushion in multicolored matte glazes, 2¾", Black Mark #1, $16.00 – $26.00. (B) Cat card suit pincushion (cushion holder is heart-shaped) in multicolored luster and shiny glazes, 2½", Red Mark #1, $16.00 – $26.00.

Plate 416. (A) Dog and cart pincushion or cache pot in multicolored luster glazes, 3¼", Red Mark #1, $12.00 – $20.00. (B) Dog with pipe on bus pincushion or cache pot in multicolored luster and shiny glazes, 2¼", Red Mark #1, $12.00 – $20.00.

Plate 417. Three little pig pincushions. (A) 3",
Black Mark #1 and Blind Mark #2. (B) 3¼", Black
Mark #1 and Blind Mark #2. (C) 3", Red Mark #1
and Blind Mark #2. $18.00 – $28.00 each.

Plate 418. Bird and tree pincushion in multicolored matte glazes, 2",
Red Mark #2, $13.00 – $22.00.

Plate 419. Rhino pincushion in blue luster glaze, 2",
Black Mark #1, $15.00 – $25.00.

Plate 420. (A) Dog pincushion
in multicolored luster and shiny
glazes, 2½", Red Mark #1 and
Blind Mark #2, $16.00 –
$26.00. (B) Doghouse pincush-
ion in multicolored luster and
shiny glazes, 2½", Black Mark
#38 and Blind Mark #1, $16.00
– $26.00.

Plate 421. (A) Donkey pincushion in multicolored shiny glazes, 3¼", Red Mark #1 and Blind Mark #2, $12.00 – $20.00. (B) Similar piece made as an ashtray, 2¾", Red Mark #1 and Blind Mark #1, $12.00 – $20.00.

Plate 422. Pincushion sewing kits with scissors, tape, and thimbles marked "JAPAN." (A) Telephone with letters spelling pincushion backwards, in white and multicolored shiny glazes, 6½", $20.00 – $30.00. (B) Dog in multicolored shiny glazes, 5½", $15.00 – $25.00. (C) Telephone in multicolored shiny glazes, 6½", $25.00 – $35.00.

Plate 423. Girlie pincushion sewing kit in multicolored shiny glazes, 5½", Red Mark #1, $25.00 – $35.00.

⚞ Planters and Cache Pots ⚟

Planters have drainage holes and cache pots do not. *Cache* is French for "hiding place," and the theory is that cache pots are meant to hold a liner pot, but many are too small for this. The smaller ones were often sold as plant rooters. In this book, all plant pots without drain holes are referred to as cache pots.

A display of prize-winning cactus plants from the Scappoose, Oregon, Garden Club in 1939. Cactus cultivation was very popular during the Depression, and lots of cache pots were sold as cactus holders. This picture illustrates their popularity.

Plate 424. (A) Dutch boy cache pot in multicolored shiny glazes, 5¾", Black Mark #1. (B) Dutch boy with swan cache pot in multicolored shiny glazes, 5½", Black Mark #1. $12.00 – $22.00 each.

Plate 425. Pair of Dutch boy cache pots in green luster with multicolored matte and shiny glazes, 4¼", Black Mark #1 and Blind Mark #2, $12.00 – $20.00 each.

Plate 426. Two Colonial gentlemen cache pots. (A) Yellow luster and multicolored shiny glazes, 4½", Black Mark #1 and Blind Mark #1. (B) Multicolored matte and shiny glazes, 5¼", Black Mark #1. $12.00 – $22.00 each.

Plate 427. (A) Gentleman with bouquet cache pot in multicolored shiny glazes, 4", Red Mark #2, $12.00 – $22.00. (B) Similar figurine, 4½" Black Mark #2. $8.00 – $15.00.

Plate 428. (A) Pierrot cache pot in multicolored luster and shiny glazes, 6¼", Black Mark #1, $12.00 – $22.00. (B) Pierrot cache pot in multicolored luster and shiny glazes, 5¾", Black Mark #1 and Blind Mark #1, $12.00 – $22.00.

Plate 429. Goldcastle boy and girl cache pot in multicolored luster and shiny glazes, 6", Blue Mark #43, $18.00 – $28.00.

Plate 430. Gentlemen trio cache pot in black and white shiny glazes, 4", Black Mark #1, $18.00 – $28.00.

Plate 431. (A) Gentlemen trio cache pot in multi-colored shiny glazes, 4¾", Black Mark #1 and Blind Mark #1, $18.00 – $28.00. (B) Swan with girl cache pot in multicolored luster and shiny glazes, 4", Red Mark #2, $12.00 – $22.00.

Plate 432. Girl and dog with toothache cache pot in multicolored shiny glazes, 5¾", Red Mark #21A, $22.00 – $32.00.

Plate 433. (A) Girl and dog cache pot in multicolored shiny glazes, 4¾", Red Mark #33, $22.00 – $32.00. (B) Maruyama girl cache pot in amber luster and multicolored matte glazes, 3¾", Red Mark #65, $22.00 – $28.00.

Plate 434. Pixie and log cache pot in brown and pink shiny glazes, 6" wide, Gold Label #60, $10.00 – $18.00.

Plate 435. Pixie cache pot in multicolored matte glazes, one of several similar styles in this shape and size, 3¾", Blue Mark #34, $10.00 – $18.00.

Plate 436. (A) Pixie cache pot in multicolored shiny glazes, 5¼", Black Mark #1, $12.00 – $22.00. (B) Pixie cache pot in multicolored luster and matte glazes, 4¼", Blue Mark #34, $12.00 – $22.00.

Plate 437. (A) Little devil cache pot in multicolored shiny glazes, 3", Black Mark #1, $12.00 – $22.00. (B) Pixie cache pot in multicolored shiny glazes, 3", Black Mark #1, $12.00 – $22.00.

Plate 438. Three swan cache pots in multicolored shiny glazes. (A) 4", Black Mark #2, $12.00 – $20.00. (B) Pictured in the 1932 Sears & Roebuck Catalog for $.59, 3¾", Black Mark #1, $12.00 – $22.00. (C) 2¼", Red Mark #20, $12.00 – $22.00.

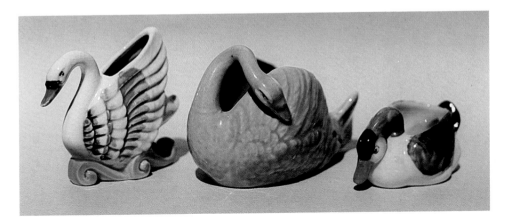

Plate 439. Large swan cache pot in multicolored shiny glazes, 7¾", Black Mark #17, $15.00 – $28.00.

Plate 440. (A) Swan cache pot in celadon glaze, 5½", Black Mark #84, $12.00 – $22.00. (B) Dog with lolling tongue cache pot in cream shiny glaze, 3½", Black Mark #1, $12.00 – $20.00.

Plate 441. Two duck cache pots in yellow and multicolored shiny glazes. (A) 5½", Black Mark #1, $15.00 – $25.00. (B) 3¾", Black Mark #1, $12.00 – $20.00.

Plate 442. Three duck cache pots in multicolored shiny glazes showing a similarity between Occupied Japan and Made in Japan pieces. (A) 3", Black Mark #33 and Made in Occupied Japan, $15.00 – $25.00. (B) 3½", Black Mark #1, $10.00 – $20.00. (C) Maruyama, 4¼", Green Mark #65, $15.00 – $25.00.

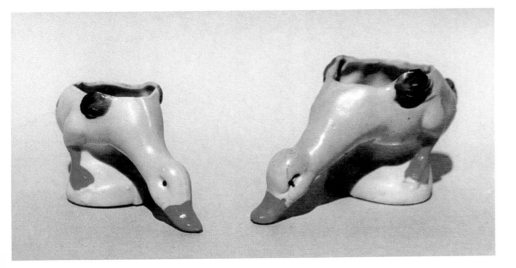

Plate 443. Pair of duck cache pots in multicolored shiny glazes. (A) 2", Black Mark #2, $10.00 – $20.00. (B) 2½", Black Mark #2, $12.00 – $25.00.

Plate 444. Dog with food dish cache pot in multicolored shiny glazes, 3", Black Mark #2, $12.00 – $22.00.

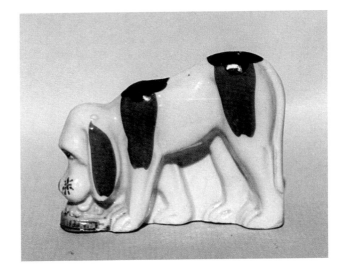

Plate 445. (A) Doghouse cache pot in multicolored shiny glazes, 3¼", Black Mark #1 with original price $.39 cents, $10.00 – $18.00. (B) Doghouse cache pot in multicolored shiny glazes, 5¼", Black Mark #1, $12.00 – $22.00.

Plate 446. Big Scottie cache pot in multicolored shiny glazes, 7½", Black Mark #1, $18.00 – $28.00.

Plate 447. Dog cache pot in green and white semi-matte glaze, 5", Black Mark #33, $12.00 – $18.00.

Plate 448. (A) Double dog cache pot in blue and white semi-matte glaze, 4½", Black Mark #1, $12.00 – $22.00. (B) Dog cache pot in orange and white semi-matte glaze, 2¼", Black Mark #2, $10.00 – $18.00.

Plate 449. Big bad wolf cache pot in multicolored shiny glazes, 5", Black Mark #1, $12.00 – $25.00.

Plate 450. Horse and cowboy cache pot in multicolored shiny glaze, 7" wide, Black Mark #1, $12.00 – $25.00.

Plate 451. Frog and turtle cache pot in multicolored shiny glazes, 4"
Black Mark #1 and Blind Mark #76, $15.00 – $28.00.

Plate 452. Two double frog
cache pots in multicolored
shiny glazes. (A) 4½", Black
Mark #90. (B) 4½", Black
Mark #1. $15.00 – $28.00
each.

Plate 453. Two colossal elephant
cache pots in multicolored shiny
glazes, 9" tall, Black Mark #2, $25.00
– $50.00 each.

Plate 454. Two elephant cache pots. (A) Cream and multicolored shiny glazes, 6", Black Mark #1, $20.00 – $35.00. (B) Gray and multicolored crackle glazes, 6½", Black Mark #1, $20.00 – $35.00.

Plate 455. Two elephant cache pots. (A) Multicolored shiny glazes, 3½", Black Mark #24, $12.00 – $20.00. (B) Blue shiny glazes, 3¾", Black Mark #2 with original price $.15, $12.00 – $20.00.

Plate 456. Two elephant cache pots in orange matte glaze. (A) 2¾", Black Mark #1, $10.00 – $20.00. (B) 5", Red Mark #90, $12.00 – $20.00.

Plate 457. Two elephant cache pots. (A) Celadon glaze, 5¼", Black Mark #1, $12.00 – $22.00. (B) Green shiny glazes, 3½", Blind Mark #1, $12.00 – $22.00.

Plate 458. Elephant cache pot, 5¼", Black Mark #91, $8.00 – $15.00.

Plate 459. Pair of wishing well cache pots in multicolored shiny glazes, 5". (A) Black Mark #1. (B) Black Mark #2. $10.00 – $18.00 each.

Plate 460. Pair of Maruyama planters in multicolored shiny glazes, both Black Mark #65 with "N" in circle. (A) 3¾". (B) 3½". $12.00 – $22.00 each.

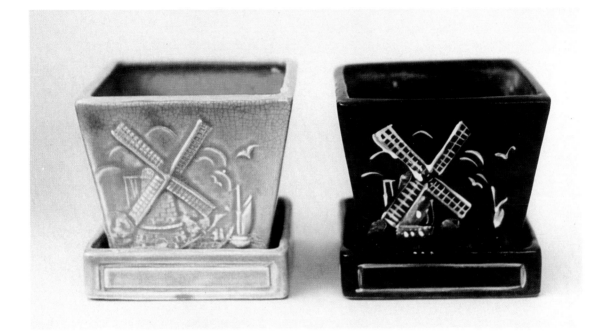

Plate 461. Pair of Maruyama planters in multicolored shiny glazes, 3¼", both Black Mark #65 with "N" in circle, $12.00 – $22.00 each.

Plate 462. (A) Maruyama planter in multicolored shiny glazes, 3¼", Black Mark #65, $12.00 – $22.00. (B) Planter in multicolored shiny glazes, 3¼", Black Mark #1, $10.00 – $18.00.

Plate 463. Pair of planters in blue shiny glaze. (A
3¼", Black Mark #1. (B) 3¼", Black Mark #1
$10.00 – $18.00 each.

Plate 464. Goldcastle planter in multicolored shiny glazes, 5", Red Mark #44,
$15.00 – $25.00.

Plate 465. Pair of bluebird planters in multicol
ored shiny glazes. (A) 3½", Red Mark #1
$10.00 – $18.00. (B) 4¾", Red Mark #1
$12.00 – $22.00.

✒ Powder Boxes ✒

Some early ads referred to these as "powder puff boxes," but collectors today seem to prefer "powder boxes."

Plate 466. Colonial powder box in multicolored shiny glazes, pictured in a 1920s Larkin Catalog for $2.00 with premium, 7", Red Mark #1, $100.00 – $150.00.

Plate 467. (A) Lady powder box in turquoise and multicolored shiny glazes, 5", Red Mark #32, $60.00 – $125.00. (B) Goldcastle Pierrot powder box in yellow luster glaze, 4½", Red Mark #43, $55.00 – $80.00.

Plate 468. (A) Flapper powder box in orange and multicolored luster and shiny glazes, 4¼", Red Mark #24, $45.00 – $75.00. (B) Clown powder box in multicolored luster and shiny glazes (almost identical to a Noritake inkwell, but the piece pictured here has no well — a good example of blanks being altered for different functions), 4½", Black Mark #1, $35.00 – $65.00.

Plate 469. Colonial lady powder box in blue shiny glaze, 7", Black Mark #2, $25.00 – $40.00.

Plate 470. Goldcastle colonial lady powder box in white shiny glaze, 6¾", Red Mark #44, $18.00 – $30.00.

Plate 471. Colonial couple powder or candy box in white shiny glaze, 6¾" Black Mark #1, $15.00 – $25.00.

Plate 472. (A) Vanity or ring box in multicolored luster glazes, 1¾", Black Mark #1, $10.00 – $18.00. (B) Chick powder box in tan luster with yellow matte figures, 3¼", Black Mark #1, $15.00 – $22.00.

Plate 473. (A) Powder box in orange matte glaze with multicolored bamboo motif, 3½" wide, Red Mark #1, $10.00 – $18.00. (B) Card suit powder box or candy in blue shiny glaze, 3½" wide, Black Mark #92, $15.00 – $30.00.

⊿ Satsuma ⊿

True Satsuma was made for centuries in Japan, and the Kyoto area is closely identified with this type of decoration. The older, traditional pieces are very different from the Satsuma we think of today with the dark brown base glaze, enameling, and raised faces and figures outlined in gold. This type of decoration is usually from this century, and is more properly called Satsuma-style, because it was widely imitated throughout Japan and exported to the United States. Sometimes Satsuma-style is called Thousand Faces. The male figures with halos are disciples of Buddha called Rakan, and the little dog finials are called Shi Shi. The pieces pictured here are from this century.

Plate 474. Satsuma-style ashtrays. (A) Swan, 3¾", Red Mark #1. (B) Elephant, 2", Red Mark #1. (C) Lion, 3", Red Mark #1. $15.00 – $25.00 each.

Plate 475. Satsuma-style ashtray with tan luster glaze, 3¼", Red Mark #2, $10.00 – $20.00.

Plate 476. Satsuma-style seated lady ashtray or pin tray, 2¾", Black Mark #1, $15.00 – $25.00.

Plate 477. Satsuma-style bonbon dish with reed handle, 8" wide, Red Mark #93, $20.00 – $45.00.

Plate 478. Pair of Satsuma-style dog cache pots, 5¼", Black Mark #1, $25.00 – $35.00 each.

Plate 479. Goldcastle Satsuma-style two-piece incense burner in multicolored matte glazes, 5¾", Red Mark #44, $12.00 – $22.00.

Plate 480. Two Satsuma-style incense burners, both with Red Mark #1. (A) 6¼". (B) 5¾". $15.00 – $25.00 each.

Plate 481. (A) Goldcastle Satsuma-style incense burner, 5¼", Red Mark #44, $15.00 – $25.00. (B) Satsuma incense burner, 4¼", Red Mark #1, $10.00 – $15.00.

Plate 482. Satsuma-style incense burner, 6¼", no Mark but red Japanese characters, $20.00 – $35.00.

Plate 483. Satsuma-style lamp base showing side with hole for cord, 6", Red Mark #1, $50.00 – $95.00.

Plate 484. Buddha Satsuma-style lamp with incense holder (these were sold both with and without the little domed cage that fit over the burner bowl), 5¾", Red Mark #1, $25.00 – $55.00.

Plate 485. Satsuma-style lemon server, 6", Red Mark #1, $20.00 – $35.00.

Plate 486. Satsuma-style liquor barrel in green shiny glaze with moriage motif, 9" tall, Red Mark #94, $50.00 – $75.00 as pictured ($60.00 – $100.00 with tray or wooden stand).

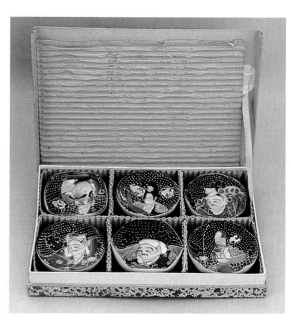

Plate 487. Set of Satsuma salts or small bowls in original box, each 2" wide, no Mark but red Japanese characters, set $100.00 – $200.00.

Plate 488. Satsuma-style teapot, 5½", Black Mark #63, $35.00 – $75.00.

Plate 489. Satsuma-style teapot in green shiny glaze with gold luster blown-out elephants, dragon spout, and elephant knob, 5½", Black Mark #1, $35.00 – $75.00.

Plate 490. (A) Satsuma-style vase, 6", Black Mark #1, $18.00 – $35.00. (B) Satsuma-style vase, 5¾", Black Marks #1 and 40, $18.00 – $35.00.

Plate 491. Satsuma-style vase, 6¼", Black Mark #1 with incised numeral "2," $18.00 – $35.00.

⚜ Shoes ⚜

Shoes continue to be popular because so many collectors buy them for what they are, regardless of the country of origin.

Plate 492. Shoe in multicolored luster glazes, 5¾", no Mark, $10.00 – $20.00.

Plate 493. Shoe in maroon and multicolored matte glazes, 2½", Red Mark #1, $10.00 – $20.00.

Plate 494. Shoe in orange and multicolored matte glazes, 3¾", Red Mark #2, $10.00 – $20.00.

Plate 495. (A) Shoe with mice in multicolored shiny glazes, 2½", Black Mark #1, $10.00 – $20.00. (B) Shoe with dog and cat in multicolored shiny glazes, 3¼", Red Mark #1, $12.00 – $22.00.

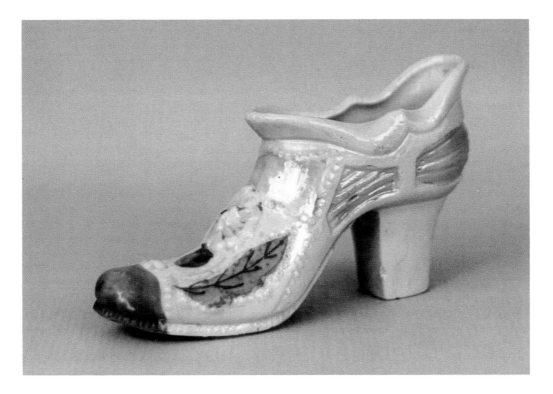

Plate 496. Shoe in multicolored luster glazes, 2¾", Black Mark #2, $12.00 – $22.00.

☙ Snack Sets ☙

These were originally called "refreshment sets" or "tea and toast sets," then later "snack sets" or "TV sets."

Plate 497. Card suit snack set in blue luster with green bird and white cherry blossom and Mt. Fuji motif, plates 7" wide with Red Mark #1, cups no Mark, set $75.00 – $125.00.

Detail of cup in card suit snack set.

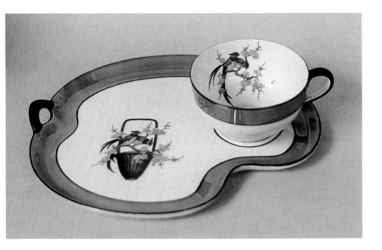

Plate 498. Noritake snack set in blue luster with white shiny glaze and multicolored decal motif, plate 8½" wide with no Mark, cup Green Mark #53, $18.00 – $48.00.

Plate 499. (A) Snack set in green and multicolored luster glazes, 8" wide, plate and cup both Red Mark #94, $15.00 – $25.00. (B) Snack set in white and tan luster glazes with arts and crafts motif, 7¼" wide, plate and cup both Black Mark #1, $15.00 – $25.00.

⚜ Souvenir and Scenic Plates ⚜

Usually made to hang on the wall, these colorful souvenirs are a combination of hand-painted motifs and decals.

Plate 500. (A) Oregon state plate, 6¼", Silver Label #60, $5.00 – $12.00. (B) Oregon state plate, 6", Red Mark #3A, $5.00 – $12.00.

Plate 501. (A) Las Vegas plate, 5½", Red Mark #95, $5.00 – $12.00. (B) Rock City plate, 4", Red Mark #96, $5.00 – $12.00.

Plate 502. (A) San Francisco plate, 4", Black Mark #97, $5.00 – $12.00. (B) California state plate, a souvenir of my parents' trip in 1953 or 1954, 8¼", Gold Label #59, $5.00 – $12.00.

Plate 503. (A) Washington state plate, 6¼", Red Mark #1, $5.00 – $12.00. (B) Scenic plate, 7¼", Red Mark #1, $5.00 – $12.00.

Plate 504. Scenic plate in multicolored luster glazes, 8½", Red Mark #25, $18.00 – $32.00.

ᨑ Sunbonnet Girls ᨐ

Most of the hats are not sunbonnets, but that's what collectors call them anyway.

Plate 505. Two Sunbonnet girl cache pots in tan luster with multicolored shiny glaze figures, 4½", Black Mark #1, $20.00 – $35.00 each.

Plate 506. Two Sunbonnet girl figurines in multicolored shiny glazes. (A) 4¾", Red Mark #1. (B) 5", Black Mark #1. $20.00 – $35.00 each.

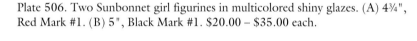

Plate 507. Sunbonnet girl napkin ring in multicolored shiny glazes, 4¼", Black Mark #2, $15.00 – $25.00.

Plate 508. Sunbonnet girl shakers in multicolored shiny glazes. (A) Single shaker, 3¾", Black Mark #2, $10.00 – $15.00. (B) Single shaker, 3", Black Mark #2, $10.00 – $15.00. (C) Salt and pepper, 3¼", Black Mark #2, pair $15.00 – $30.00.

Plate 509. Sunbonnet girl shakers in multicolored shiny glazes. (A) and (C) Salt and pepper, 2", Black Mark #2, pair $15.00 – $30.00. (B) Single shaker, 3¼", $10.00 – $15.00.

Plate 510. Sunbonnet girl salt and pepper sets in multicolored shiny glazes, 3¼". (A) Black Mark #2. (B) Red Mark #2. Each pair $15.00 – $30.00.

Plate 511. Sunbonnet girls on fish shakers in multicolored shiny glazes, the far left one is inscribed "Oceanlake Ore," 3", all Black Mark #2, $10.00 – $15.00 each.

⚐ Tea and Coffee Items ⚐

Teapots are like the song, "short and stout," with definite spouts. The tall thin pots with the long spouts are demitasses and the tall pots with the pitcher-like pouring spouts are chocolate pots.

Plate 512. Tea set in cream and white semi-matte glazes with gold luster accents, similar to Noritake's "White and Gold" pattern and from the same time period, all with Red Mark #50. (A) Teapot with tile, tile 5½" wide. (B) Biscuit barrel, 7¾". (C) Cheese and cracker set, 10½" wide. (D) Cream and sugar on tray, 8" wide. $125.00 – $155.00 for the set.

Plate 513. Tea set in white shiny glaze with multicolored luster butterfly motif, plate 7¼", Red Mark #98, $50.00 – $60.00 as pictured, $105.00 – $150.00 complete with four or six plates, cups, and saucers.

Plate 514. Tea set in tan luster and white shiny glazes, pictured in the 1927 Sears & Roebuck Catalog with blue and white glazes at $4.25 for service for six, plate 7¼" wide, Red Mark #1, cups no Mark, $50.00 – $60.00 as pictured, $105.00 – $150.00 complete with four or six plates, cups, and saucers.

Plate 515. Tea set in multicolored luster glazes, plate 7½" wide, Black Mark #1, $50.00 – $60.00 as pictured, $105.00 – $150.00 complete with four or six plates, cups, and saucers.

Plate 516. Tea set in orange shiny glaze with white cherry blossom motif, pictured in the 1927 Sears & Roebuck Catalog with different glazes for $4.25 per set, plate 7¼" wide, Blue Mark #52, cups and saucers no Mark, $50.00 – $60.00 as pictured, $105.00 – $150.00 complete with four or six plates, cups, and saucers.

Plate 517. Teapot, cream, and sugar in white shiny glaze with gold luster bamboo motif, 7", no Mark but Japanese characters, set $35.00 – $65.00.

Plate 518. Top: Lithophane cup and saucer in white shiny glaze with gold luster bamboo motif, no Mark, $10.00 – $28.00. Bottom: Detail of lithophane, which is a raised figure stamped right into the body of the piece so the light shining through makes a picture.

Plate 519. Teapot and hot water set on tray in multicolored luster glazes (a good example of the differences between amber, tan, and gold), 6" wide, Red Mark #28, $75.00 – $125.00.

Plate 520. (A) Teapot on tile in red and white shiny glazes, 6", Red Mark #12A, $38.00 – $62.00. (B) Matching cream and sugar on tray, 6¾" wide, Red Mark #12A, set $46.00 – $68.00.

Plate 521. (A) Teapot on tile in cream and multicolored shiny glazes, 7", Red Mark #1, $38.00 – $62.00. (B) Teapot on tile in orange and multicolored shiny glazes, 7", Red Mark #1, $38.00 – $62.00.

Plate 522. Two teapots with multicolored crackle glaze, 6¾", Red Mark #28, $30.00 – $50.00 each.

Plate 523. (A) Teapot in tan and multicolored luster glazes with flowers and butterfly, 6¾", Red Mark #56, $28.00 – $43.00. (B) Teapot in tan and blue luster glaze with bird, 5¾", Black Mark #2, $28.00 – $43.00.

Plate 524. (A) Teapot in blue and multicolored luster glazes with blown-out birds, 6¼", Black Mark #56, $28.00 – $43.00. (B) Teapot in blue and multicolored luster glazes with scenic motif, 5¾", Blind Mark #1, $28.00 – $43.00.

Plate 525. (A) Teapot in multicolored shiny glazes with floral motif, 7", Black Mark #1, $28.00 – $43.00. (B) Six-sided teapot in yellow and multicolored shiny glazes, 7¾", Red Mark #24, $28.00 – $43.00.

Plate 526. (A) Teapot in blue luster glaze with checkerboard motif, 5", Black Mark #10, $28.00 – $43.00. (B) Teapot in blue and multicolored luster glazes with floral motif, 7", Mark obscured, $28.00 – $43.00.

Plate 527. (A) Teapot in yellow and multicolored luster glazes, 5¾", Red Mark #99, $28.00 – $43.00. (B) Goldcastle checkerboard teapot in multicolored luster glazes, 6", Black Mark #43, $28.00 – $43.00.

Plate 528. Teapot in multicolored luster glazes with windmill motif, pictured in the 1933 Sears & Roebuck Catalog with assorted decorations for $.49, 7¾", Red Mark #24, $28.00 – $43.00.

Plate 529. (A) Teapot in multicolored crackle glazes, 5", Black Mark #1, $20.00 – $40.00. (B) Teapot in cream and multicolored shiny glazes, 5¼", $18.00 – $28.00.

Plate 530. (A) Individual teapot on plate in blue and white shiny glazes, 3", Black and Yellow Label with "JAPAN" and Japanese characters, $10.00 – $20.00. (B) Individual teapot in brown shiny glaze with enameling, 3¼", Yellow Mark #104, $10.00 – $20.00.

Plate 531. (A) Teapot with Majolica-type multicolored motif, 4½", Black Mark #1 and Blind Mark #1, $28.00 – $55.00. (B) Elephant teapot in brown shiny glaze on brown body, 5", White Mark #2, $20.00 – $35.00.

Plate 532. (A) Elephant teapot in tan and multicolored luster glazes, 7½", Black Mark #1, $38.00 – $75.00. (B) Camel teapot in orange and multicolored luster glazes, 6", Black Mark #1, $38.00 – $75.00.

Plate 533. (A) Goldcastle teapot in blue and multicolored shiny glazes with gold luster dragon spout and knob, 7¾", Red Mark #43, $38.00 – $65.00. (B) Camel teapot in yellow and multicolored shiny glazes, pictured in the 1931 Sears & Roebuck Catalog for $1.00, 6", Red Mark #50, $38.00 – $75.00.

Plate 534. Coffee server on warmer in brown and multicolored shiny glazes on brown clay body, 10½", Blind Mark #1, $20.00 – $40.00.

Plate 535. Coffee set in white shiny glaze with pink flower decals and traveling case, case 13" wide, Gold Label #111, $200.00 – $250.00.

Plate 536. Demitasse pot, cream, and sugar in gold luster with white flowers, 7½", Red Mark #101, $30.00 – $40.00 as pictured; $50.00 – $70.00 for complete set with pot, cream and sugar, and four or six plates, cups, and saucers.

⚰ Toothbrush Holders ⚰

In one sense, anything with a big enough opening could be used as a toothbrush holder, but we have to limit ourselves to those objects that really look as if they might have been intended for that purpose.

Plate 537. "Dwarf" toothbrush holder or cache pot in multicolored shiny glazes with no Disney trademark, 3½", Black Mark #1, $18.00 – $28.00.

Plate 538. (A) Girl toothbrush holder in multicolored luster and shiny glazes, 5¾", no Mark and no incised numbers so it could be Japanese or German, $55.00 – $65.00. (B) Bisque naughty girl toothbrush holder inscribed "Course I'm a girl Don't you see my hair ribbon," 4¼", Black Mark #38, $55.00 – $65.00.

Plate 539. Three musician toothbrush holders in multicolored luster and shiny glazes, 4¼" – 4½", Blind Mark #1, $55.00 – $65.00 each.

Plate 540. Oriental figural toothbrush holder in multicolored shiny glazes, 5¼", Black Mark #3A, $55.00 – $65.00.

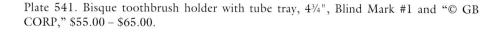

Plate 541. Bisque toothbrush holder with tube tray, 4¾", Blind Mark #1 and "© GB CORP," $55.00 – $65.00.

Plate 542. (A) Bisque boy with bouquet toothbrush holder, 5", Black Mark #2, $55.00 – $65.00. (B) Boy and dog toothbrush holder in multicolored semi-matte glazes, 6¼", Black Mark #1, $40.00 – $55.00.

Plate 543. Dutch boy toothbrush holder in multicolored luster and shiny glazes, 4¾", Black Mark #1, $55.00 – $65.00.

Plate 544. Clown toothbrush holder in multicolored shiny and matte glazes, 5", Black Mark #2, $40.00 – $55.00.

Plate 545. Pig toothbrush holder in multicolored shiny glazes, 3", Black Mark #2, $55.00 – $65.00.

Plate 546. (A) Duck toothbrush holder in multicolored shiny glazes, 4¾", Red Mark #11, $55.00 – $65.00. (B) Dog toothbrush holder in multicolored shiny glazes, 4", Mark obscured, $55.00 – $65.00.

Plate 547. Duck toothbrush holder in multicolored luster and shiny glazes, pictured in the 1934 Sears & Roebuck Catalog as Taisho Ware for $.10, 4½" Red Mark #32B, $55.00 – $65.00.

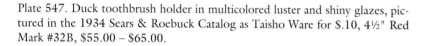

Plate 548. (A) Dog toothbrush holder in brown and multicolored semi-matte glazes, 6¼", Red Mark #1 and Blind Mark #1, $50.00 – $75.00. (B) Bonzo toothbrush holder in blue luster glaze, 5¾", Red Mark #1, $115.00 – $220.00.

⚐ Toothpick Holders ⚐

Here again, collectors of different categories might label these items match holders, but probably not nut cups.

Plate 549. (A) Man with cart toothpick holder in multicolored shiny glazes, 3½", Black Mark #102, $18.00 – $30.00. (B) Bird and flowers toothpick holder in multicolored shiny glazes, 5¼", Red Mark #1, $20.00 – $35.00. (C) Oriental man toothpick holder in multicolored shiny glazes, 3¾", Red Mark #66B, $18.00 – $28.00.

Plate 550. Blue-faced dog toothpick holder or cache pot in multicolored semi-matte glazes, 3¼", Red Mark #103, $18.00 – $28.00.

Plate 551. Toothpick holder in blue luster glaze, 3", Red Mark #74, $18.00 – $30.00.

☄ Useful Objects ☄

Here's the really neat stuff — the novelties and interesting dishes that make collecting so much fun!

Plate 552. Bird Feeder in multicolored shiny glazes, 3¼", Black Mark #1, $18.00 – $28.00.

Plate 553. Calendar with day/date/month cards in blue and multicolored shiny glazes, 2¾" Black Mark #2, $25.00 – $40.00.

Celery dishes were sold both with and without sets of matching salt dips, so if you find a celery by itself, don't pass it up because it may not have had salts with it.

Plate 554. Celery and salt set in multicolored luster glazes, 13" wide, all Black Mark #1, $28.00 – $65.00.

Plate 555. Noritake celery dish in multicolored shiny glazes, 12" wide, Red Mark #53, $30.00 – $60.00.

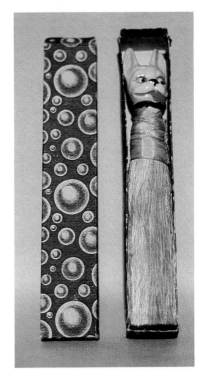

Plate 556. Dog clothes brush in multicolored shiny glazes in original box, 8", box Black Mark #1, brush Red Mark #1, $28.00 – $52.00.

Plate 557. Two cups and saucers that were a gift to the owner's great aunt from the Japanese delegation to the 1893 Columbian Exposition in Chicago. (A) Pink shiny glaze with gold luster accents, no Mark but Japanese characters, $20.00 – $35.00. (B) Kutani-style Geisha girls and scenes from Japan in multicolored shiny glazes, no Mark but Japanese characters, $20.00 – $35.00.

Plate 558. Pair of jointed bisque dolls, boy 3¾", girl 3½" (costumes cover the Marks), $25.00 – $50.00 each.

Plate 559. Peacock hatpin, hors d'oeuvre, or joss stick holders in multicolored semi-matte glazes, 3¾". (A) Red Mark #1. (B) Red Mark #66. $25.00 – $50.00 each.

Plate 560. Man wearing sombrero hatpin or hors d'oeuvre holder in white luster and multicolored shiny glazes, 4¾", Red Mark #2, $25.00 – $35.00.

Plate 561. Maruyama elephant hatpin or hors d'oeuvre holder in green shiny glaze, 3½", Red Marks #65, $20.00 – $30.00.

Plate 562. Noritake marmalade set in amber and multicolored luster glazes with butterfly finial, 5" tall, spoon and pot Green Mark #26, plate no Mark, $55.00 – $85.00.

In the old catalogs, the sets that we call "muffineers" today were often referred to as "berry sugar and cream sets" or "waffle sets."

Plate 563. Muffineer set in multicolored crackle glazes, 7", Black Mark #1, $35.00 – $65.00.

Plate 564. Dutch people muffineer set in multicolored luster glazes, 5¾", Red Mark # 25, $55.00 – $95.00.

Plate 565. Mugs in multicolored luster glazes, 3", Red Mark #25, $8.00 – $18.00 each.

Plate 566. Cat napkin ring in pink shiny glaze, 3", Black Mark #1, $21.00 – $26.00.

Plate 567. Dutch boy perfume in multicolored luster and shiny glazes, 3½", Red Mark #1, $50.00 – $85.00.

Plate 568. Maruyama place card holder in multicolored shiny glazes, 1½", Red Mark #65, $27.00 – $35.00.

Plate 569. Goldcastle potpourri or pomander box (has holes by feet and on lid, so it can't be a cigarette box) in multicolored shiny glazes with bird finial, 3¼", Red Mark #44, $20.00 – $30.00.

Plate 570. (A) Elephant razor safe in gray matte glaze with multicolored luster motif, 3", Red Mark #1, $28.00 – $38.00. (B) Donkey razor safe in multicolored matte glazes, 3¾" Black Mark #1, $18.00 – $28.00.

Plate 571. (A) Ring basket in blue shiny glaze, 2¼", Green Mark #1, $5.00 – $10.00. (B) Ring basket in white shiny glaze, 2¼", Black Mark #2, $5.00 – $10.00.

Plate 572. Two ring trays in multicolored luster and shiny glazes inscribed "JUST MARRIED." (A) 3½", Black Mark #1. (B) 3¾", no Mark. $12.00 – $20.00 each.

Plate 573. Footed sauce boat and plate in multicolored luster and shiny glazes, 3" tall, Black Mark #1, $25.00 – $55.00.

Plate 574. Noritake covered gourd-shaped sauce dish in yellow and multicolored shiny glazes, 5", dish and ladle Blue Mark #26, $35.00 – $75.00.

Plate 575. Covered gourd-shaped sauce dish in blue and multicolored luster glazes, 5", dish and plate Red Mark #1, $35.00 – $75.00.

Plate 576. String holder girl in multicolored shiny glazes, 6½", Black Mark #1 with "60868W" and Japanese characters, $38.00 – $48.00.

Plate 577. Syrup pitcher with liner bowl in multicolored luster and shiny glazes, tray 7" wide, Black Mark #11, $36.00 – $48.00.

Plate 578. Syrup pitcher in yellow and amber luster with multicolored floral motif, liner plate 6½" wide, Red Mark #25, $36.00 – $48.00.

Plate 579. Clown thermometer in gray luster and multicolored shiny glazes, 4¾", Red Mark #1, $25.00 – $35.00.

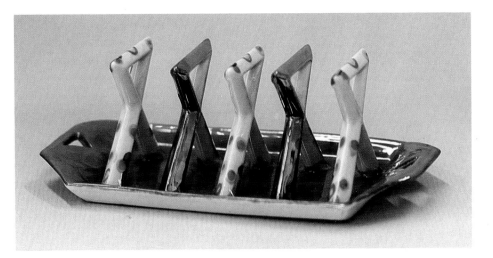

Plate 580. Toast rack in blue luster and multicolored shiny glazes, pictured in the 1931 Sears & Roebuck Catalog as a "Toast or Napkin Rack" for $1.00, 7½" long, Red Mark #1, $25.00 – $50.00.

Plate 581. Noritake toast rack in multicolored luster glazes, 5¾" long, Red Mark #53, $50.00 – $75.00.

Plate 582. Toast rack in tan and blue luster, 5¼" long, Black Mark #100, $25.00 – $50.00.

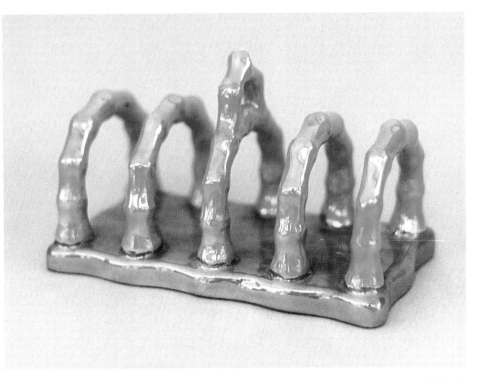

⚔ Vases ⚔

The Japanese were prolific vase producers. They made every shape and size, from the most petite bud vase to the largest urns.

Plate 583. Two Indian and tree vases as pictured in a pre-World War II Butler Bros. Catalog for $.65 wholesale/$1.00 – $1.50 retail. (A) Tan and multicolored luster glazes, 7¼", Black Mark #1, $50.00 – $100.00. (B) Multicolored shiny glazes, 7¼", Black Mark #1, $50.00 – $100.00.

Plate 584. Bear and tree vase in multicolored luster and shiny glazes, 7¼", Black Mark #1, $50.00 – $75.00.

Plate 585. Dog and owl tree vase in multicolored luster and shiny glazes, base has dimple for lamp fitting, 7", Black Mark #1, $50.00 – $75.00.

Plate 586. Bird vase in multicolored luster and shiny glazes, as pictured in a pre-World War II Butler Bros. Catalog for $.65 wholesale/$1.00 – $1.50 retail, 7¼", Black Mark #1, $40.00 – $65.00.

Plate 587. Noritake bird vase in amber and multicolored luster glazes, 5¼", Green Mark #26, $100.00 – $150.00.

Plate 588. Bird vase in multicolored shiny glazes, 6¼", Black Mark #1, $30.00 – $55.00.

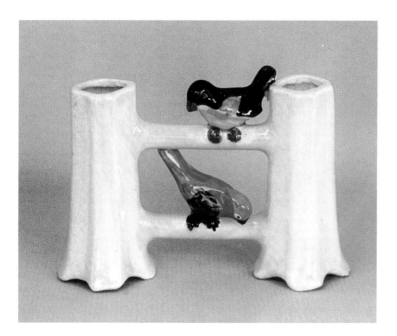

Plate 589. Bird vase in multicolored semi-matte glazes, 3¾", Blind Mark #1, $20.00 – $40.00.

Plate 590. Stork vase in multicolored shiny glazes, 4¼", Black Mark #1, $20.00 – $45.00.

Plate 591. (A) Stork vase in multicolored shiny glazes, 7", Black Mark #2 with original price $.79, $22.00 – $35.00. (B) Duck vase or cache pot in multicolored shiny glazes, 6¼", Black Mark #3, $18.00 – $32.00.

Plate 592. Frog and flower vase in tan luster and multicolored shiny glazes, 3¾", Black Mark #1, $22.00 – $32.00.

Plate 593. Two frog vases in multicolored shiny glazes, pictured in the 1933 Sears & Roebuck Catalog for $.49 "for flowers or growing vines," 6¾", Blind Mark #1, $25.00 – $55.00 each.

Plate 594. Dog on book vase in multicolored semi-matte glazes, 3¾", Blind Mark #1, $12.00 – $18.00. Often these were sold with cigarette lighters inserted in the vase.

Plate 595. Mask vase or cache pot in red and multicolored semi-matte glazes, 4", Red Mark #23, $20.00 – $45.00.

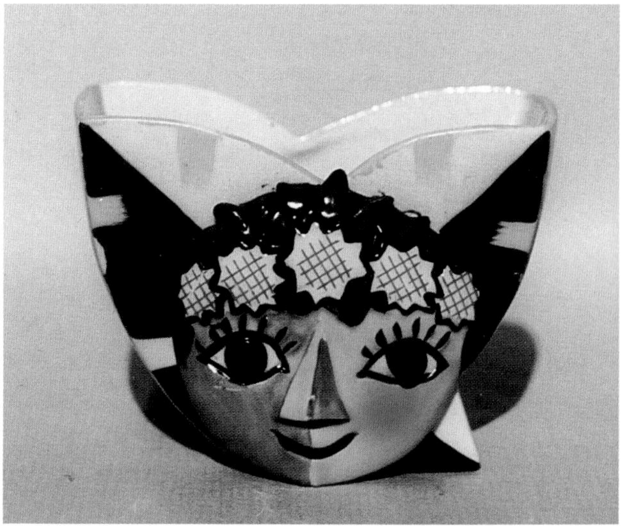

Plate 596. Face vase or cache pot in multicolored shiny glazes, 3¼", Red Mark #23, $20.00 – $45.00.

Plate 597. Three colonial lady vases in multicolored matte and luster glazes. (A) 4½", Red Mark #18, $20.00 – $30.00. (B) 7¼", Red Mark #2, $25.00 – $35.00. (C) (also made as an incense burner) 5¾", Red Mark #2, $27.00 – $37.00.

Plate 598. Lady head vase with detachable parasol in white shiny glaze with gold luster accents, head 5" incised with "N" in a circle, parasol Red Mark #2, $25.00 – $45.00.

Plate 599. Lady head vase in multicolored shiny glazes, 3½", Black Mark #1, $22.00 – $35.00.

Plate 600. Lady head vase in white shiny glaze, 7¼", Black Mark #1, $12.00 – $22.00. (A similar cache pot was produced in America with the "U.S.A." mark. Which was the knockoff?)

Plate 601. Girl bud vase in multicolored shiny glazes, 6¼", Black Mark #1 and Blind Mark #38, $20.00 – $30.00.

Plate 602. (A) Pixie on swing tree vase, 4¼", Red Mark #2, $15.00 - $28.00. (B) Boy and dog tree vase, 2¾", Black Mark #51, $8.00 - $18.00.

Plate 603. Tulip vase in multicolored shiny glazes, 5¾", Black Mark #1, $10.00 – $20.00.

Plate 604. Boot vase in German Beer Stein-style, 8¼", Black Mark #23, $25.00 – $60.00.

Plate 605. Pair of vases in multicolored semi-matte glazes, showing both back and front motifs, very similar to Hand Painted Nippon vases, pre-World War II pieces from the Akiyama Store, 10¼", Blue Mark #105, $90.00 – $100.00 each, $150.00 – $160.00 pair.

Plate 606. Vase in blue and multicolored crackle glaze, a pre-World War II piece from the Akiyama Store, 9¾", Gold Mark #1 with Japanese characters, $65.00 – $85.00.

Plate 607. Tall vase in blue and amber luster with multicolored scenic motif and dimple for lamp fitting, a pre-World War II piece from the Akiyama Store, 9½", Black Mark #1, $30.00 – $45.00.

Plate 608. (A) Urn in blue and white matte glazes, 7½", Black Mark #1, $20.00 – $35.00. (B) Basket vase in multicolored shiny glazes, 7½", Black Mark #35, $25.00 – $45.00. (C) Textured scenic vase in multicolored shiny glazes, 7½", Blind Mark #1, $25.00 – $45.00.

Plate 609. (A) Pierced vase with bird motif in multicolored shiny glazes, 7½", Blind Mark #1, $18.00 – $28.00. (B) Footed vase in multicolored shiny glazes, 8½", Black Mark #1, $18.00 – $28.00.

Plate 610. (A) Shell flower bowl in multicolored shiny glazes, 5", Black Mark #1, $22.00 – $32.00. (B) Cornucopia vase with cupids in multicolored shiny glazes, 10", Black Mark #1, $22.00 – $32.00.

Plate 611. (A) Bud vase in multicolored shiny glazes with floral motif, 5", Brown Mark #85, $15.00 – $25.00. (B) Bud vase in multicolored shiny glazes with bird motif, 5", Blind Mark #1, $18.00 – $25.00.

Plate 612. (A) Blue vase with moriage Golden Gate Bridge motif, 5", Black Mark #63, $25.00 – $50.00. (B) Gray vase with moriage dragon motif, 5", Black Mark #52, $20.00 – $35.00.

Plate 613. (A) Rustic vase in multicolored shiny glazes, 5¾", Black Mark #3A, $15.00 – $20.00. (B) Red heart vase with cupid in multicolored shiny glazes, 4¼", Black Mark #106, $20.00 – $35.00.

Plate 614. Vase with mottled purple and silver luster glazes, 9¾", Silver Mark #1, $20.00 – $30.00.

Plate 615. Three-handled vase in multicolored shiny glazes, a pre-World War II piece from the Akiyama Store, 7¼", no Mark, $75.00 – $105.00.

Plate 616. Tokanabe-type vase in multicolored matte glazes with dimple for lamp fitting, 9½", Blind Mark #1, $25.00 – $35.00.

Plate 617. Hanging vase in blue and multicolored shiny glazes, 6½", Black Mark #1, $55.00 – $70.00.

Plate 618. Hanging vase in turquoise semi-matte glaze, 4", Black Mark #1, $55.00 – $70.00.

Plate 619. Hanging vase in multicolored luster and shiny glazes, 4¼", Black Mark #1, $55.00 – $70.00.

Wall Pockets

Wall pockets have taken off as a collectible category, but they are still fairly plentiful.

Plate 620. Japanese lady "Banko Ware" wall pocket in multicolored matte glazes, pictured in the 1922 Sears & Roebuck Catalog for $.89, 9", Blind Mark #1, $35.00 – $65.00.

Plate 621. (A) Majolica-type floral wall pocket in multicolored shiny glazes, 6¾", Black Mark #1, $25.00 – $55.00. (B) Majolica-type bird wall pocket in multicolored shiny glazes, 6½", Black Mark #1, $20.00 – $35.00.

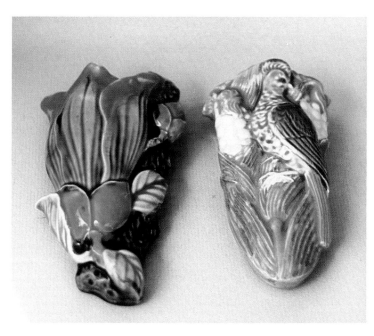

Plate 622. Floral wall pocket in multicolored shiny glazes, 6¼", Blind Mark #1, $20.00 – $45.00.

Plate 623. Bird wall pocket in brown and multicolored shiny glazes, 6¾", Blind Mark #1, $25.00 – $45.00.

Plate 624. Bird and bamboo wall pocket in multicolored shiny glazes, 6½", Black Mark #3A, $18.00 – $28.00.

Plate 625. Swan wall pocket in multicolored shiny glazes, 6¾", Black Mark #1 and Blind Mark #1, $18.00 – $28.00.

Plate 626. Bird wall pocket in multicolored shiny glazes, 7½", Blind Mark #1, $18.00 – $35.00.

Plate 627. Duck wall pocket in multicolored shiny glazes, 5½", Green Mark #107, $18.00 – $28.00.

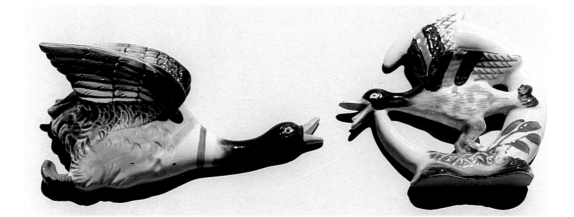

Plate 628. Flying duck wall pockets in multicolored shiny glazes. (A) 10½", Black Mark #1, $18.00 – $28.00. (B) 7¾", Black Mark #1, $18.00 –$28.00.

Plate 629. Three flying duck wall pockets in multicolored shiny glazes showing the similarity between Made in Japan and Made in Occupied Japan pieces. (A) 9¼", Blind Mark #1, $18.00 – $28.00. (B) 6", marked "Made in Occupied Japan," $18.00 – $28.00. (C) 6¼", marked "Made in Occupied Japan" with Blind Mark #1, $18.00 – $28.00.

Plate 630. Cat and clock wall pocket in multicolored semi-matte glazes, 3¾", Red Mark #11, $18.00 – $28.00.

⧏ Water Sets ⧐

Sometimes called "tumble-ups," all of the water sets pictured here are pre-World War II. The first five are pieces from the Akiyama Store.

Plate 631. Kinkozan water set in blue and orange shiny glazes, jug 6" with Red Mark #49, glass 4" with Red Mark #1, $50.00 – $75.00.

Plate 632. Kinkozan water set in blue and cream shiny glazes, jug 6" with Red Mark #49, glass 4" with Red Mark #2 and Japanese characters, $50.00 – $75.00.

Plate 633. Kinkozan water set in blue and brown shiny glazes, jug 6¼" with Red Mark #49, glass 4" with Red Mark #49, $50.00 – $75.00.

Plate 634. Kinkozan water set in black and multicolored shiny glazes, jug 6½" with Red Mark #49, glass 4" with Red Mark #1, $50.00 – $75.00.

Plate 635. Kinkozan water set in red and multicolored shiny glazes, jug 6¼" with Red Mark #49, glass 4" with Red Mark #49, $50.00 – $75.00.

Plate 636. Water set in cream semi-matte glaze with cobalt bamboo motif, jug 6", $50.00 – $75.00.

Plate 637. Water set in amber and multicolored luster glazes, pictured in a pre-World War II Butler Bros. Catalog with similar decoration for $.65 whole-sale/$1.00 – $1.50 retail, jug 6¼" with Red Mark #1, glass 4" with Red Mark #1, $50.00 – $75.00.

⚔ Cobalt Glass ⚔

The Japanese made a lot of very interesting pieces of glass with antimony (metal) holders. Although they are not ceramics, they are interesting "go-withs." There is a candy dish similar to the first one pictured in the 1934 Sears & Roebuck Catalog for $1.00, so we know they were made at least that far back! Here are a couple of examples:

Plate 638. Covered candy, 8", metal holder Marked Made in Japan, glass liner no Mark, $25.00 – $75.00.

Plate 639. Salt dip, 2¼", metal holder Marked Made in Japan, glass no Mark, $8.00 – $15.00.

Selections from a 1960s Pacific Orient Imports Catalog

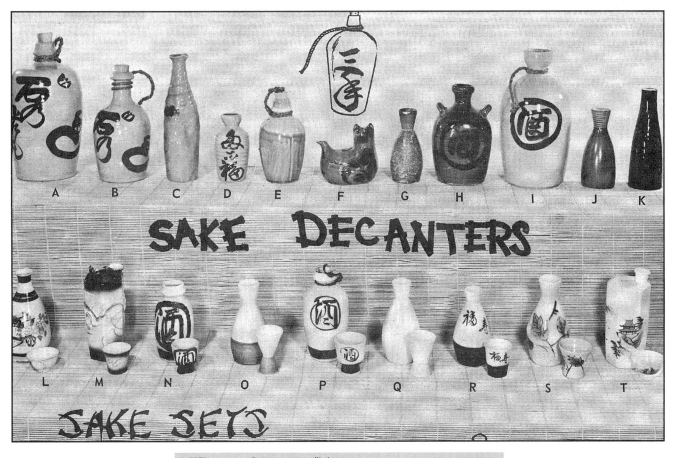

A-9971	Oyster gray, metallic brown character, 10-½"	$24.00 dz.
B-9972	Oyster gray, metallic brown character, 8-½"	$12.00 dz.
C-9978	Beige black pine branch, 9"	$ 9.00 dz.
D-9980	Oyster gray, metallic brown character, 5"	$ 3.00 dz.
E-10069	Acid beige in gray, 4"	$ 6.60 dz.
F-19G	Metallic brown badger, 5-½"	$ 4.80 dz.
G-44G	Mocern red-rust, 7"	$ 9.00 dz.
H-52G	Khaki metallic brown character, 9-½"	$16.50 dz.
I-53G	Oyster gray metallic brown character, 5-½"	$24.00 dz.
J-166P	Red and beige, 7"	$ 6.60 dz.
K-167P	Green and black, 5-½"	$ 8.40 dz.
L-9578	7 pc. red and gold set, 6"	$15.00 dz.
M-9628	Black-blue gray dragon, 5"	$21.00 dz.
N-9708	Gray metallic brown character, 7 pc. set, 5"	$15.00 dz.
O-10045	Porcelain white bamboo design 7 pc. set, 6"	$19.50 dz.
P-7G	Oyster gray metallic brown character, 7 pc. set, 5"	$24.00 dz.
Q-41G	Porcelain white, 7 pc. set, 5"	$18.00 dz.
R-56G	Modern white and black 7pc. set, 5-½"	$18.00 dz.
S-94G	Metallic blue-brown design 7 pc. set, 6"	$30.00 dz.
T-94G	Porcelain white temple design 6"	$30.00 dz.

All prices are wholesale and in dozen lots, except where price is listed for per one item or per one set.

Selections from a 1965 – 66 Norcrest Fine Gifts and China Catalog

Page 6

NOVEL NORCREST MUGS, DECANTERS AND PARTY ACCESSORIES

C-134 3.60 dz.   C-183 2 asst. 7.80 dz.   C-271 3.60 dz.   C-280 3 asst. 6.60 dz.   C-284 2.70 dz.

C-296 2.70 dz.   C-321 4 asst. 3.00 dz.   C-339 4 asst. 5.40 dz.   C-340 4 asst. 2.40 dz.   C-341 3 asst. 3.00 dz.   C-342 4.80 dz.   C-345 4.80 dz.   C-349 4 asst. 2.40 dz.

C-350 4.80 dz.   C-353 6.00 dz.   C-354 6.00 dz.   C-357 3.00 dz.   C-358 6 asst. 2.40 dz.   C-362 4 asst. 3.00 dz.   C-367 4 asst. 4.20 dz.   C-368 3 asst. 4.80 dz.   C-377 3 asst. 8.40 dz.   C-382 4 asst. 7.20 dz.

C-384 4 asst. 2.40 dz.   C-394 3 asst. 2.40 dz.   C-440 6.00 dz. C-442 6.00 dz.   C-444 6 asst. 3.60 dz.   C-344 6.00 dz.   C-447 3 asst. 3.60 dz.   C-448 3 asst. 3.00 dz.

C-443 6.60 dz.   C-150 6.60 dz.   L-280 10.80 dz.   L-281 12.00 dz.   J-764 8.40 dz.   J-381 6.60 dz.   J-545 Musical 27.00 dz.

Page 10

NORCREST PLANTERS ARE PROFIT MAKERS

E-895 7.20 dz.   E-865 2 asst. 7.20 dz.   E-841 6.00 dz.   E-901 12.00 dz.   E-869 9.60 dz.   E-705 6.60 dz.   E-736 7.20 dz.   E-875 2 asst. 9.60 dz.

E-886 2 asst. 8.40 dz.   E-872 9.00 dz.   E-821 3 asst. 10.80 dz.   E-880 7.80 dz.   E-654 7.20 dz.   E-755 6.60 dz.

E-885 12.00 dz.   E-721 2 asst. 7.80 dz.   E-833 2 asst. 7.20 dz.   E-734 7.80 dz.   A-906 7.80 dz.   E-727 15.00 dz.   E-881 3 asst. 4.80 dz.   E-651 2 asst. 12.00 dz.

E-871 12.00 dz.   E-724 8.40 dz.   E-897 7.80 dz.   E-753 2 asst. 7.80 dz.   E-818 2 asst. 10.20 dz.   E-840 12.00 dz.   E-839 16.50 dz.   A-857 9.60 dz.

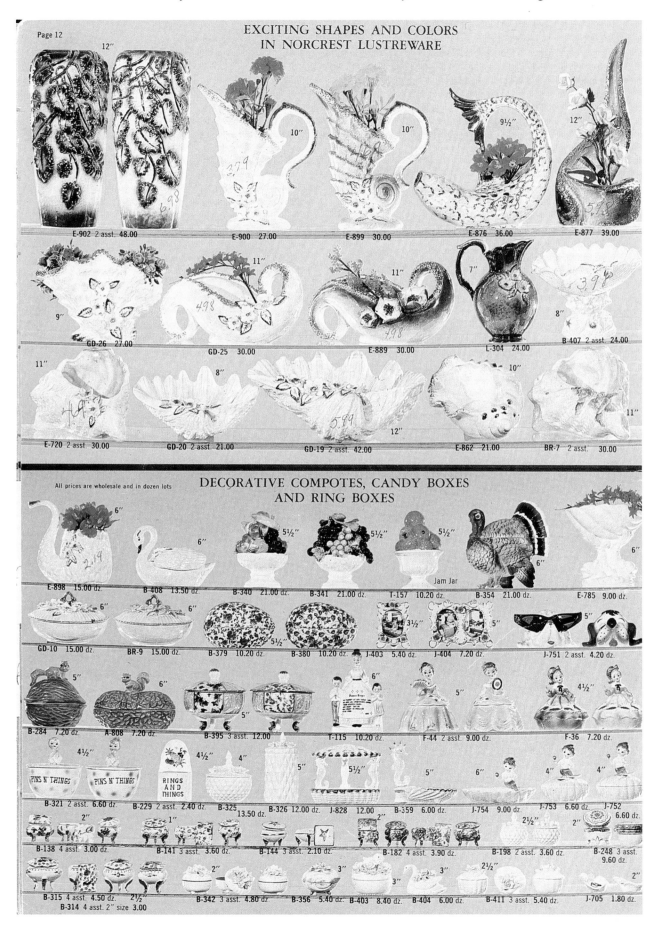

Page 12

EXCITING SHAPES AND COLORS
IN NORCREST LUSTREWARE

E-902 2 asst. 48.00   E-900 27.00   E-899 30.00   E-876 36.00   E-877 39.00

GD-26 27.00   GD-25 30.00   E-889 30.00   L-304 24.00   B-407 2 asst. 24.00

E-720 2 asst. 30.00   GD-20 2 asst. 21.00   GD-19 2 asst. 42.00   E-862 21.00   BR-7 2 asst. 30.00

All prices are wholesale and in dozen lots

DECORATIVE COMPOTES, CANDY BOXES
AND RING BOXES

E-898 15.00 dz.   B-408 13.50 dz.   B-340 21.00 dz.   B-341 21.00 dz.   T-157 10.20 dz.   B-354 21.00 dz.   E-785 9.00 dz.

Jam Jar

GD-10 15.00 dz.   BR-9 15.00 dz.   B-379 10.20 dz.   B-380 10.20 dz.   J-403 5.40 dz.   J-404 7.20 dz.   J-751 2 asst. 4.20 dz.

B-284 7.20 dz.   A-808 7.20 dz.   B-395 3 asst. 12.00   T-115 10.20 dz.   F-44 2 asst. 9.00 dz.   F-36 7.20 dz.

PINS N' THINGS   PINS N' THINGS   RINGS AND THINGS

B-321 2 asst. 6.60 dz.   B-229 2 asst. 2.40 dz.   B-325 13.50 dz.   B-326 12.00 dz.   J-828 12.00   B-359 6.00 dz.   J-754 9.00 dz.   J-753 6.60 dz.   J-752 6.60 dz.

B-138 4 asst. 3.00 dz.   B-141 3 asst. 3.60 dz.   B-144 3 asst. 2.10 dz.   B-182 4 asst. 3.90 dz.   B-198 2 asst. 3.60 dz.   B-248 3 asst. 9.60 dz.

B-315 4 asst. 4.50 dz.   B-314 4 asst. 2" size 3.00   B-342 3 asst. 4.80 dz.   B-356 5.40 dz.   B-403 8.40 dz.   B-404 6.00 dz.   B-411 3 asst. 5.40 dz.   J-705 1.80 dz.

Selections from a 1965 – 66 Norcrest Fine Gifts and China Catalog

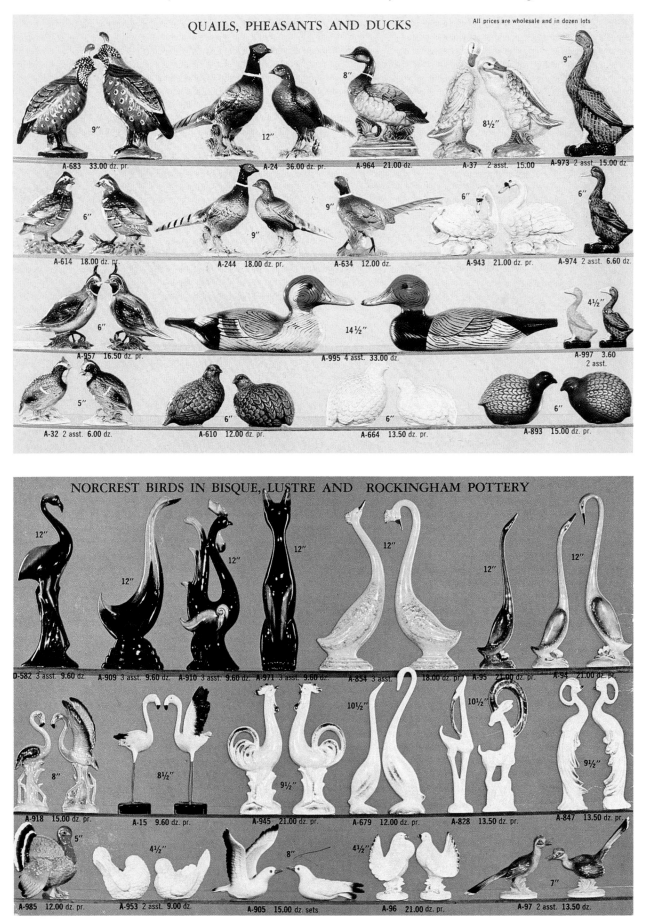

QUAILS, PHEASANTS AND DUCKS

All prices are wholesale and in dozen lots

9″

12″

8″

8½″

9″

A-683 33.00 dz. pr.   A-24 36.00 dz. pr.   A-964 21.00 dz.   A-37 2 asst. 15.00   A-973 2 asst. 15.00

6″

9″

9″

6″

6″

A-614 18.00 dz. pr.   A-244 18.00 dz. pr.   A-634 12.00 dz.   A-943 21.00 dz. pr.   A-974 2 asst. 6.60 dz.

6″

14½″

4½″

A-957 16.50 dz. pr.   A-995 4 asst. 33.00 dz.   A-997 3.60 2 asst.

5″

6″

6″

6″

A-32 2 asst. 6.00 dz.   A-610 12.00 dz. pr.   A-664 13.50 dz. pr.   A-893 15.00 dz. pr.

NORCREST BIRDS IN BISQUE, LUSTRE AND ROCKINGHAM POTTERY

12″

12″

12″

12″

12″

12″

12″

D-582 3 asst. 9.60 dz.   A-909 3 asst. 9.60 dz.   A-910 3 asst. 9.60 dz.   A-971 3 asst. 9.60 dz.   A-854 3 asst. 18.00 dz. pr.   A-95 21.00 dz. pr.   A-94 21.00 dz. pr.

8″

8½″

9½″

10½″

10½″

9½″

A-918 15.00 dz. pr.   A-15 9.60 dz. pr.   A-945 21.00 dz. pr.   A-679 12.00 dz. pr.   A-828 13.50 dz. pr.   A-847 13.50 dz. pr.

5″

4½″

8″

4½″

7″

A-985 12.00 dz. pr.   A-953 2 asst. 9.00 dz.   A-905 15.00 dz. sets   A-96 21.00 dz. pr.   A-97 2 asst. 13.50 dz.

Selections from a 1965 – 66 Norcrest Fine Gifts and China Catalog

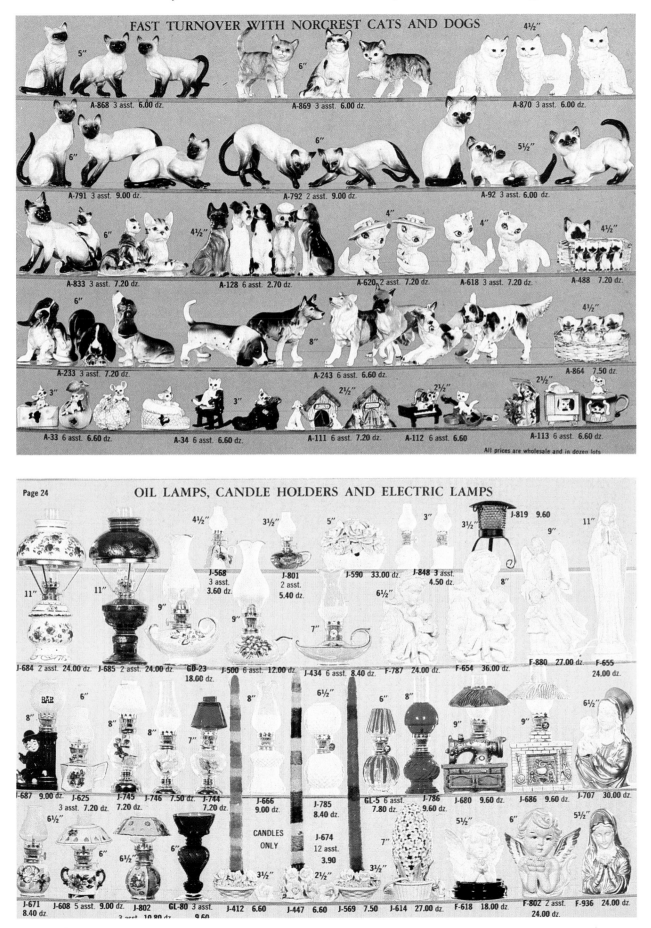

FAST TURNOVER WITH NORCREST CATS AND DOGS

5"   4½"
A-868 3 asst. 6.00 dz.   6"   A-869 3 asst. 6.00 dz.   A-870 3 asst. 6.00 dz.

6"   6"   5½"
A-791 3 asst. 9.00 dz.   A-792 2 asst. 9.00 dz.   A-92 3 asst. 6.00 dz.

6"   4½"   4"   4"   4½"
A-833 3 asst. 7.20 dz.   A-128 6 asst. 2.70 dz.   A-620 2 asst. 7.20 dz.   A-618 3 asst. 7.20 dz.   A-488 7.20 dz.

6"   8"   4½"
A-233 3 asst. 7.20 dz.   A-243 6 asst. 6.60 dz.   A-864 7.50 dz.

3"   3"   2½"   2½"   2½"
A-33 6 asst. 6.60 dz.   A-34 6 asst. 6.60 dz.   A-111 6 asst. 7.20 dz.   A-112 6 asst. 6.60   A-113 6 asst. 6.60 dz.

All prices are wholesale and in dozen lots

Page 24   **OIL LAMPS, CANDLE HOLDERS AND ELECTRIC LAMPS**

4½"   3½"   5"   3"   3½"   J-819 9.60   11"
J-568   J-801   J-590 33.00 dz.   J-848 3 asst.   9"
3 asst.   2 asst.   4.50 dz.   8"
3.60 dz.   5.40 dz.   6½"

11"   11"   9"   9"   7"
J-684 2 asst. 24.00 dz.   J-685 2 asst. 24.00 dz.   GD-23 18.00 dz.   J-500 6 asst. 12.00 dz.   J-434 6 asst. 8.40 dz.   F-787 24.00 dz.   F-654 36.00 dz.   F-880 27.00 dz.   F-655 24.00 dz.

BAB   6"   8"   6½"   6"   8"   6½"
8"   8"   8"   7"   9"   9"
J-687 9.00 dz.   J-625   J-745   J-746 7.50 dz.   J-744   J-666   J-785   GL-5 6 asst.   J-786   J-680 9.60 dz.   J-686 9.60 dz.   J-707 30.00 dz.
3 asst. 7.20 dz.   7.20 dz.   7.20 dz.   9.00 dz.   8.40 dz.   7.80 dz.   9.60 dz.

6½"   6"   6½"   7"   5½"   6"   5½"
J-674   12 asst.
3.90
J-671   J-608 5 asst. 9.00 dz.   J-802   GL-80 3 asst.   3½"   J-412 6.60   2½"   J-447 6.60   3½"   J-569 7.50   J-614 27.00 dz.   F-618 18.00 dz.   F-802 2 asst.   F-936 24.00 dz.
8.40 dz.   3 asst. 10.80 dz.   9.60   CANDLES ONLY   24.00 dz.

SHAMROCK DECORATED GIFTWARES ADD UP TO LUCKY SALES FOR YOU

⑬

Music Boxes

6"

4"

9"

(Planter)

BK-128 (Bank)
16.50 dz/pc

F-506 42.00 dz/pc

F-526 42.00 dz/pc

F-508 2/ast 8.40 dz/pc

F-509 2/ast 9.00 dz/pc

E-178 24.00 dz/pc

E-180 12.00 dz/pc

TA-16 (Prepack "Shamrock Boy & Girl" Kitchenware Assortment includes 18 pieces, 7 assorted items) 27.00 per assortment

4½"

9"

TA-22 (Prepack "Springs of Shamrocks" Tableware Assortment includes 18 pieces, 7 assorted items) 24.00 per assortment

PR-16 (Prepack "Lustre Shamrocks" Decorator Assortment includes 22 pieces, 13 assorted items) 27.00 per assortment

LIVEN UP THE KITCHEN WITH COLORFUL CANDY BOXES AND JAM JARS

7"

5"

6½"

T-1 42.00 dz/pc

B-379 19.50 dz/pc

B-380 19.50 dz/pc

B-771 24.00 dz/pc

T-186 27.00 dz/pc

T-187 48.00 dz/pc

4½"

5½"

4"

5"

T-8 24.00 dz/pc

T-23 24.00 dz/pc

T-46 12.00 dz/pc

T-79 24.00 dz/pc

T-178 12.00 dz/pc

T-195 12.00 dz/pc

T-509 15.00 dz/pc

T-545 18.00 dz/pc

5½"

4"

4½"

T-221 4/ast 15.00 dz/pc

T-527 3/ast 15.00 dz/pc

T-423 4/ast 18.00 dz/pc

EVERYBODY LOVES PURPLE COWS AND OTHER ANIMALS TO DECORATE THE KITCHEN

(14)

T-77 72.00 dz/pc   T-480 45.00 dz/pc   T-487 66.00 dz/pc   T-71 75.00 dz/pc   T-163 69.00 dz/pc   T-164 72.00 dz/pc

T-78 18.00 dz/pr   H-317 15.00 dz/pr   H-170 15.00 dz/pr   H-197 12.00 dz/pr   T-75 18.00 dz/pr   H-232 9.00 dz/pr   H-233 9.00 dz/pr   H-308 18.00 dz/pr

REVIEW OF COMING EVENTS IN GIFTWARES:
TA-1 (Prepack assortment featuring "Mizz Blossom the Cow")

T-73

T-79 18.00 dz/pc   BK-134 18.00 dz/pc   BK-36 18.00 dz/pc   T-72 (Butter Dish) 30.00 dz/pc   T-76 (Jam Jar) 21.00 dz/pc

TA-1 (Brand new assortment unavailable before catalog goes to press, write to us for details)

T-540 (3/pc Creamer/Salt/Pepper) 12.00 dz/st   L-415 (Creamer) 9.00 dz/pc   L-434 (Creamer) 18.00 dz/pc   T-74 (Sugar/creamer) 36.00 dz/st

UNIVERSAL APPEAL WITH VIOLET DESIGN GIFTWARES

TA-24 (Prepack "Spring Violets" Kitchenware Assortment includes 21 pieces, 8 assorted items) 29.00 per assortment

MA-14 (Prepack "Violets for Mother" Assortment includes 19 pieces, 7 assorted items) 48.00 per assortment

VT-8 (Prepack "Teatime Violets" Hand painted Assortment includes 20 pieces, 4 assorted items) 32.00 per assortment

(58)

SEND FOR OUR $50 ASSORTMENT OF BEST SELLING BANKS

9½"   10½"   6"   5½"   6"

| A-489 | 42.00 dz/pc | A-629 | 42.00 dz/pc | | BK-87 | 54.00 dz/pc | X-529 | 15.00 dz/pc | X-605 | 24.00 dz/pc | X-534 16.50 dz/pc | X-542 | 12.00 dz/pc |

7"   4½"   6½"   6½"

| A-51 | 27.00 dz/pc | A-735 15.00 dz/pc | BK-17 2/ast 24.00 dz/pc | BK-18 | 21.00 dz/pc | X-363 18.00 dz/pc | BK-86 27.00 dz/pc | BK-127 21.00 dz/pc |

6½"   5½"   5½"   5"   4½"

ALL PRICES SUBJECT TO CHANGE WITHOUT NOTICE

4"   3½"   2½"   5½"

| BK-913 | 30.00 dz/pc | A-317 | 18.00 dz/pc | BB-18 13.50 dz/pc | T-22 15.00 dz/pc | BK-28 10.20 dz/pc | BK-97 7.50 dz/pc | A-512 2/ast 6.00 dz/pc | BK-46 3/ast 6.00 dz/pc | X-487 13.50 dz/pc |

4½"   4"   5"   5"   3"

| BK-22 9.00 dz/pc | BK-23 9.00 dz/pc | BK-36 3/ast 15.00 dz/pc | A-599 3/ast 9.00 dz/pc | A-543 12/ast 6.00 dz/pc |

LET US SEND YOU OUR $50 BEST SELLING BANK ASSORTMENT

9"   6"   BK-122 36.00 dz/pc   9"

| BK-42 18.00 dz/pc | A-970 2/ast 15.00 dz/pc | BK-41 9.00 dz/pc | BK-133 3/ast 18.00 dz/pc | BK-123 3/ast 12.00 dz/pc |

BK-54 12.00 dz/pc   6½"   7"

| BK-53 13.50 dz/pc | BK-94 9.00 dz/pc | BK-102 2/ast 18.00 dz/pc | BK-77 13.50 dz/pc | BK-78 13.50 dz/pc | BK-105 4/ast 12.00 dz/pc |

6½"   5½"   5"   5"

| BK-37 3/ast 12.00 dz/pc | BK-134 15.00 dz/pc | BK-95 9.00 dz/pc | BK-96 9.00 dz/pc | BK-125 12/ast 12.00 dz/pc |

| BK-73 2/ast 18.00 dz/pc | A-491 16.50 dz/pc | BK-100 15.00 dz/pc | A-521 15.00 dz/pc | BK-99 2/ast 9.60 dz/pc | A-513 18.00 dz/pc | BK-24 15.00 dz/pc | BK-116 16.50 dz/pc | BK-117 16.50 dz/pc |

(59)

BK-246 15.00 dz/pc   BK-98 3/ast 12.00 dz/pc   BK-43 4/ast 18.00 dz/pc   BK-128 16.50 dz/pc   X-364 24.00 dz/pc

BK-82 2/ast 39.00 dz/pc   F-230 21.00 dz/pc   F-231 21.00 dz/pc   BK-92 12.00 dz/pc   BK-93 12.00 dz/pc   BK-107 15.00 dz/pc   BK-108 15.00 dz/pc   BK-232 2/ast 21.00 dz/pc

BK-132 2/ast 24.00 dz/pc   BK-181 2/ast 18.00 dz/pc   BK-81 2/ast 12.00 dz/pc   BK-138 2/ast 9.00 dz/pc   BK-126 2/ast 21.00 dz/pc   BK-113 3/ast 12.00 dz/pc   BK-35 2/ast 9.00 dz/pc

YOU'LL BE LAUGHING ALL THE WAY TO THE BANK WHEN YOU SELL FUNNY BANKS FROM NORCREST

A-299 30.00 dz/pc   A-519 24.00 dz/pc   BK-91 2/ast 18.00 dz/pc   A-154 (Figurine) 18.00 dz/pc   A-591 18.00 dz/pc   BK-298 24.00 dz/pc   BK-106 30.00 dz/pc

BK-57 18.00 dz/pc   BK-58 18.00 dz/pc   W-504 9.60 dz/pc   W-428 8.10 dz/pc   BK-84 4/ast 10.20 dz/pc

BK-73 2/ast 18.00 dz/pc   BK-10 9.60 dz/pc   BK-112 12.00 dz/pc   BK-9 4/ast 12.00 dz/pc   BK-90 2/ast 9.60 dz/pc

BK-89 10.80 dz/pc   BK-110 12.00 dz/pc   BK-111 12.00 dz/pc   BK-122 4/ast 9.60 dz/pc   BK-40 8.40 dz/pc   BK-386 9.00 dz/pc   BK-51 12.00 dz/pc

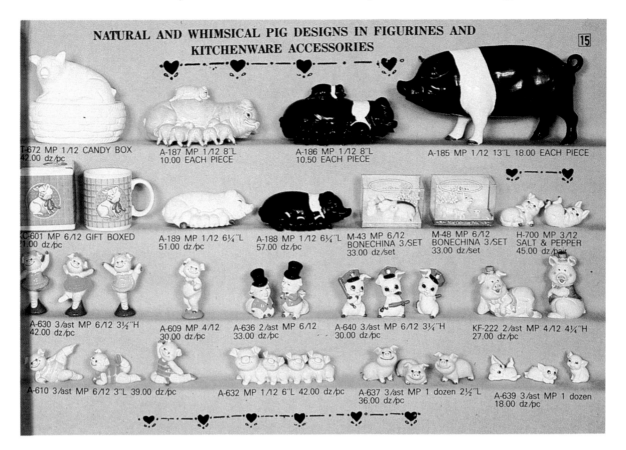

Selections from a 1989 Norcrest Fine Gifts and China Catalog

KITTY CAT AND SCOTTY DOG FIGURINES AND GIFTWARE ACCESSORIES

08 MP 1/12
TEAPOT
EACH PIECE

K-70 MP 1/12
6 3/4"H TEAPOT
10.00 EACH PIECE

TM-50 MP 1/12
7"L TEAPOT
5.50 EACH PIECE

K-230 MP 1/12
7"L TEAPOT
11.00 EACH PIECE

K-107 MP 1/12
4½"H SUGAR & CREAMER
5.50 EACH SET

K-109 MP 1/12
7½"H TEAPOT
9.00 EACH PIECE

NEW! NEW!

(NOT DISPLAYED)
K-71 SUGAR & CREAMER
MP 1/12 4"H
9.00 EACH SET

K-72 COFFEE MUG
MP 4/12 3¼"H
48.00 dz/pc

J-10 MP 3/12
3 3/4"H BELL
30.00 dz/pc

K-93 MP 4/12
24.00 dz/pc

K-162 MP 4/12
"I LIKE YOU"
24.00 dz/pc

K-158 MP 6/12
4"H FLOCKED
21.00 dz/pc

K-154 MP 2/12
5"H PHOTO FRAME
42.00 dz/pc

BK-788 MP 1/12 8"L BANK
39.00 dz/pc

2/12 2¼"L
A 3/SET

X-811 MP 6/12
3¼"H CANDLEHOLDER
27.00 dz/pc

X-810 3/ast 2 3/4"H
MP 6/12
24.00 dz/pc

K-170 2/ast 2½"H
MP 6/12
27.00 dz/pc

K-171 MP 6/12
"I LOVE YOU"
24.00 dz/pc

K-151 2/ast MP 2/12
3"H MAGNET FRAMES
30.00 dz/pc

K-150 2/ast MP 4/12
36.00 dz/pc

3/ast MP 6/12 3½"L
dz/pc

J-120 MP 6/12
MAGNET FRAME
30.00 dz/pc

K-84 2/ast MP 6/12
30.00 dz/pc

K-83 MP 6/12
FIGURINE ONLY
30.00 dz/pc

BA-551 MP 4/12
3½"H MUG
72.00 dz/pc

#4005 6/ast MP 6/12 4"H 15.00 dz/pc

MERRY CLOWN MUSIC BOXES, COIN BANKS AND FIGURINES

55

F-856 MP 1/12
9"H MUSIC BOX:
MERRY WIDOW
WALTZ 11.00 EACH

F-930 3/ast MP 1/12 8½"H
MUSIC BOX: MEMORIES
11.00 EACH PIECE

TF-930 MP 1/12 6"H
MUSIC BOX: THE
ENTERTAINER
14.00 EACH PIECE

TF-931 MP 1/12
11"H MUSIC BOX:
THE ENTERTAINER
15.00 EACH PIECE

F-854 MP 1/12
7½"H MUSIC BOX:
LIMELIGHT
11.00 EACH PIECE

F-855 MP 1/12
9½"H MUSIC BOX:
SEND IN THE
CLOWNS 11.00 EACH

98 2/ast MP 1/12 7 3/4"H
USIC BOX: SEND IN THE CLOWNS
00 EACH PIECE

F-849 MP 1/12 5"H
MUSIC BOX: SEND
IN THE CLOWNS
13.00 EACH PIECE

F-299 6/ast 5½"H MP 6/12 45.00 dz/pc

KB-632 BANK MP 4/12
33.00 dz/pc

BK-284 BANK &"H
MP 1/12
39.00 dz/pc

MP 1/12
D MUSIC BOX:
UPON A STAR
EACH PIECE

F-819 MP 1/12
WOOD MUSIC BOX:
THE ENTERTAINER
6.00 EACH PIECE

BK-29 4/ast BANKS MP 4/12 5½"H 30.00 dz/pc

CIRCUS

F-933 MP 1/12 5½"H
MUSIC BOX: SEND
IN THE CLOWNS
12.50 EACH PIECE

48

CHARMING PENGUIN GIFTWARE ACCESSORIES AND WHIMSICAL ANIMAL COIN BANKS

Norcrest CHINA CO

KB-601 MP 4/12
5¼"H COIN BANK
27.00 dz/pc

KB-602 MP 4/12
5½"H COIN BANK
27.00 dz/pc

KB-613 2/ast MP 2/12 BANKS
36.00 dz/pc

KB-614 MP 2/12
5½"H COIN BANK
36.00 dz/pc

K-43 MP 2/12
4½"H COIN BANK
42.00 dz/pc

K-664 MP 4/12
4½"H COIN BANK
36.00 dz/pc

X-311 MP 4/12
27.00 dz/pc

CM-294 MP 4/12 3½"H
21.00 dz/pc

BK-5 MP 2/12 BANK
78.00 dz/pc

K-986 MP 1/12
5¼"H JAM JAR
36.00 dz/pc

K-989 MP 6/12
SALT & PEPPER
24.00 dz/pair

K-985 MP 4/12
27.00 dz/pc

T-744 MP 1/12 12"H
COOKIE JAR
10.00 EACH PIECE

P-602 MP 6/12
3 3/4"L WALL HOOK
27.00 dz/pc

X-83 MP 6/12
TREE FRAME
36.00 dz/pc

X-309 3/ast MP 6/12 2¼"H
33.00 dz/pc

K-987 MP 6/12
3½"H TEA BELL
15.00 dz/pc

A-40 MP 6/12
33.00 dz/pc

A-41 MP 6/12
33.00 dz/pc

J-312 MP 6/12
MAGNET FRAM
36.00 dz/pc

CHARMING AND WHIMSICAL PENGUIN FIGURINES

Norcrest CHINA CO

A-42 3/ast 2"H MP 6/12
33.00 dz/pc

A-43 3/ast 2½"L MP 6/12 18.00 dz/pc

A-44 3/ast 2 3/4"L MP 6/12 33.00 dz/pc

A-45 3/ast 2 3/4"L MP 6/12 33.00 dz/pc

K-991 2½"H
NURSE
MP 4/12
30.00 dz/pc

K-992 2¼"H
GRADUATE
MP 4/12
30.00 dz/pc

K-994 2½"H
SECRETARY
MP 4/12
30.00 dz/pc

K-993 2½"H
CONCERT PIANIST
MP 4/12
30.00 dz/pc

K-995 2¼"H
TEACHER MP 4/12
30.00 dz/pc

K-996 2½"H
BATHER MP 6
30.00 dz/pc

H-45 2½"H MP 2/12
SALT & PEPPER PAIR
54.00 dz/pair

A-46 2/ast 2 3/4"H
MP 6/12
33.00 dz/pc

K-999 2/ast 2½"H MP 4/12
36.00 dz/pc

M-653 2/ast 1¼"H
MP 4/12
13.50 dz/pc

F-561 1 3/4"H
MP 1 dozen
24.00 dz/pc

F-567 2"H
MP 1 dozen
30.00 dz/pc

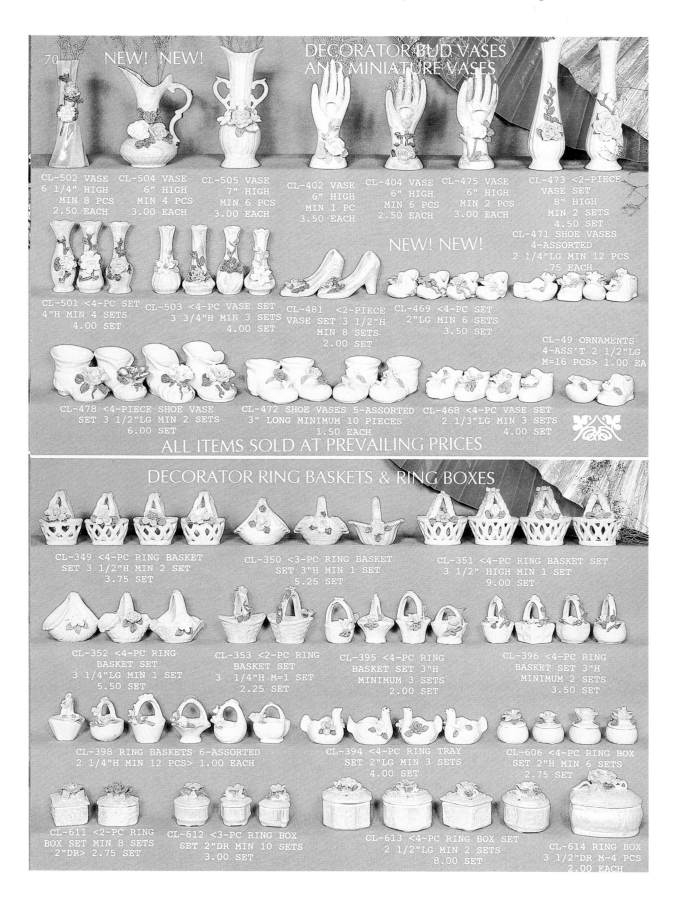

70 NEW! NEW! DECORATOR BUD VASES AND MINIATURE VASES

CL-502 VASE 6 1/4" HIGH MIN 8 PCS 2.50 EACH

CL-504 VASE 6" HIGH MIN 4 PCS 3.00 EACH

CL-505 VASE 7" HIGH MIN 6 PCS 3.00 EACH

CL-402 VASE 6" HIGH MIN 1 PC 3.50 EACH

CL-404 VASE 6" HIGH MIN 6 PCS 2.50 EACH

CL-475 VASE 6" HIGH MIN 2 PCS 3.00 EACH

CL-473 <2-PIECE VASE SET 8" HIGH MIN 2 SETS 4.50 SET

CL-471 SHOE VASES 4-ASSORTED 2 1/4"LG MIN 12 PCS .75 EACH

NEW! NEW!

CL-501 <4-PC SET 4"H MIN 4 SETS 4.00 SET

CL-503 <4-PC VASE SET 3 3/4"H MIN 3 SETS 4.00 SET

CL-481 <2-PIECE VASE SET 3 1/2"H MIN 8 SETS 2.00 SET

CL-469 <4-PC SET 2"LG MIN 6 SETS 3.50 SET

CL-49 ORNAMENTS 4-ASS'T 2 1/2"LG M=16 PCS> 1.00 EA

CL-478 <4-PIECE SHOE VASE SET 3 1/2"LG MIN 2 SETS 6.00 SET

CL-472 SHOE VASES 5-ASSORTED 3" LONG MINIMUM 10 PIECES 1.50 EACH

CL-468 <4-PC VASE SET 2 1/3"LG MIN 3 SETS 4.00 SET

ALL ITEMS SOLD AT PREVAILING PRICES

DECORATOR RING BASKETS & RING BOXES

CL-349 <4-PC RING BASKET SET 3 1/2"H MIN 2 SET 3.75 SET

CL-350 <3-PC RING BASKET SET 3"H MIN 1 SET 5.25 SET

CL-351 <4-PC RING BASKET SET 3 1/2" HIGH MIN 1 SET 9.00 SET

CL-352 <4-PC RING BASKET SET 3 1/4"LG MIN 1 SET 5.50 SET

CL-353 <2-PC RING BASKET SET 3 1/4"H M=1 SET 2.25 SET

CL-395 <4-PC RING BASKET SET 3"H MINIMUM 3 SETS 2.00 SET

CL-396 <4-PC RING BASKET SET 3"H MINIMUM 2 SETS 3.50 SET

CL-398 RING BASKETS 6-ASSORTED 2 1/4"H MIN 12 PCS> 1.00 EACH

CL-394 <4-PC RING TRAY SET 2"LG MIN 3 SETS 4.00 SET

CL-606 <4-PC RING BOX SET 2"H MIN 6 SETS 2.75 SET

CL-611 <2-PC RING BOX SET MIN 8 SETS 2"DR> 2.75 SET

CL-612 <3-PC RING BOX SET 2"DR MIN 10 SETS 3.00 SET

CL-613 <4-PC RING BOX SET 2 1/2"LG MIN 2 SETS 8.00 SET

CL-614 RING BOX 3 1/2"DR M-4 PCS 2.00 EACH

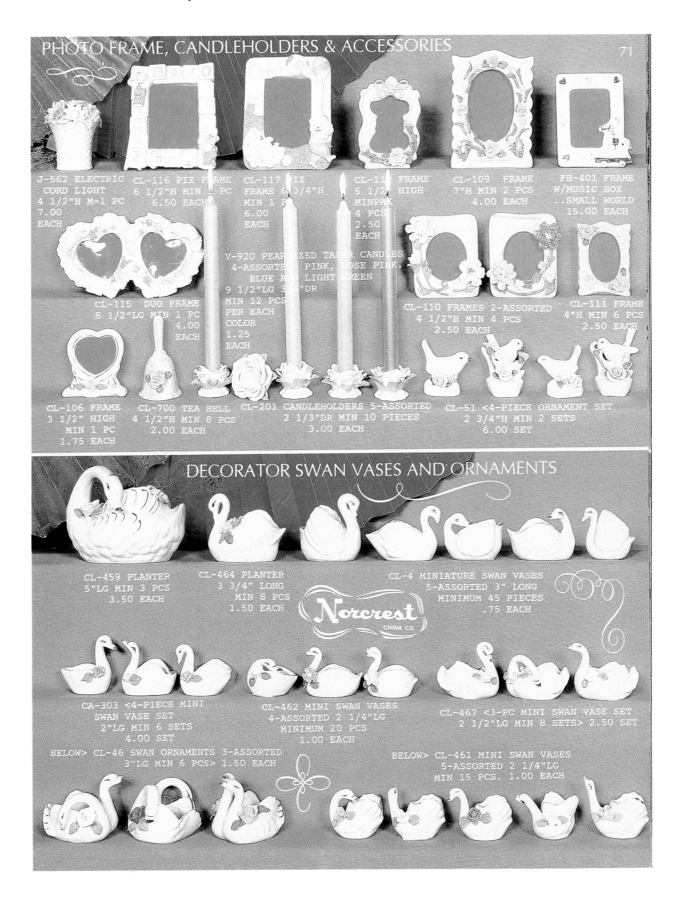

PHOTO FRAME, CANDLEHOLDERS & ACCESSORIES   71

J-562 ELECTRIC
CORD LIGHT
4 1/2"H M=1 PC
7.00
EACH

CL-116 PIX FRAME
6 1/2"H MIN 1 PC
6.50 EACH

CL-117 PIX
FRAME 6 3/4"H
MIN 1 PC
6.00
EACH

CL-11_ FRAME
5 1/2"
MINPAK
4 PCS
2.50
EACH

CL-109 FRAME
7"H MIN 2 PCS
4.00 EACH

FB-401 FRAME
W/MUSIC BOX
..SMALL WORLD
15.00 EACH

CL-115 DUO FRAME
8 1/2"LG MIN 1 PC
4.00
EACH

V-920 PEARIZED TAPER CANDLES
4-ASSORTED PINK, ROSE PINK,
BLUE AND LIGHT GREEN
9 1/2"LG 3_"DR
MIN 12 PCS
PER EACH
COLOR
1.25
EACH

CL-110 FRAMES 2-ASSORTED
4 1/2"H MIN 4 PCS
2.50 EACH

CL-111 FRAME
4"H MIN 6 PCS
2.50 EACH

CL-106 FRAME
3 1/2" HIGH
MIN 1 PC
1.75 EACH

CL-700 TEA BELL
4 1/2"H MIN 8 PCS
2.00 EACH

CL-201 CANDLEHOLDERS 5-ASSORTED
2 1/3"DR MIN 10 PIECES
3.00 EACH

CL-51 <4-PIECE ORNAMENT SET
2 3/4"H MIN 2 SETS
6.00 SET

DECORATOR SWAN VASES AND ORNAMENTS

CL-459 PLANTER
5"LG MIN 3 PCS
3.50 EACH

CL-464 PLANTER
3 3/4" LONG
MIN 8 PCS
1.50 EACH

CL-4 MINIATURE SWAN VASES
5-ASSORTED 3" LONG
MINIMUM 45 PIECES
.75 EACH

Norcrest CHINA CO.

CA-303 <4-PIECE MINI
SWAN VASE SET
2"LG MIN 6 SETS
4.00 SET

CL-462 MINI SWAN VASES
4-ASSORTED 2 1/4"LG
MINIMUM 20 PCS
1.00 EACH

CL-467 <3-PC MINI SWAN VASE SET
2 1/2"LG MIN 8 SETS> 2.50 SET

BELOW> CL-46 SWAN ORNAMENTS 3-ASSORTED
3"LG MIN 6 PCS> 1.50 EACH

BELOW> CL-461 MINI SWAN VASES
5-ASSORTED 2 1/4"LG
MIN 15 PCS. 1.00 EACH

✎ About the Author ✎

Carole Bess White is the author of another Collector Book, *The Collector's Guide to Made in Japan Ceramics,* and she has been a serious collector of Made in Japan since 1981. She is also a collector in many other categories including Depression glass, and a 1920s and 1930s movie fan.

She has started the Made in Japan Info Letter, a national newsletter on the subject of Made in Japan. She is a member of the Noritake Society, The National Cambridge Society, and a lifetime member of Portland's Rain of Glass.

Carole has worked full time in newspaper entertainment advertising for more than 20 years.

For a number of years she was also a potter, producing wheel-thrown stoneware and raku vessels.

Research on Made in Japan is a major interest of Carole's, and she will continue her studies in this area.

Les White, Ed.D., has spent many years working with photography and computers. At present he is the information technology coordinator for an area high school. Les took all the pictures in this book, except for the two or three fuzzy ones taken by Carole.

Les is not a collector of anything except computers!

The Whites reside in Portland, Oregon.

⩕ Bibliography ⩖

Andacht, Sandra. *Treasury of Satsuma.* Des Moines, IA: Wallace-Homestead Book Co., 1981.

Japan Pottery Exporters' Association, *Ceramic Japan*, Vol. 1 No. 1, Vol. 1, No. 2.

Stitt, Irene. *Japanese Ceramics of the Last 100 Years.* New York: Crown Publishers, 1974.

Van Patten, Joan. *The Collector's Encyclopedia of Noritake.* Paducah, KY: Collector Books, 1984.

Van Patten, Joan. *The Collector's Encyclopedia of Noritake*, Second Series. Paducah, KY: Collector Books, 1994.

Index

5886 **Kitchen Glassware** of the Depression Years, 5th Ed., Florence $19.95
2394 **Oil Lamps II**, Glass Kerosene Lamps, Thuro $24.95
3889 Pocket Guide to **Depression Glass**, 9th Ed., Florence $9.95
3739 Standard Encylopedia of **Carnival Glass**, 4th Ed., Edwards $24.95
3740 Standard **Carnival Glass** Price Guide, 9th Ed. $9.95
3974 Standard Encylopedia of **Opalescent Glass**, Edwards $19.95
1848 **Very Rare Glassware** of the Depression Years, Florence $24.95
2140 **Very Rare Glassware** of the Depression Years, 2nd Series, Florence $24.95
3326 **Very Rare Glassware** of the Depression Years, 3rd Series, Florence $24.95
4909 **Very Rare Glassware** of the Depression Years, 4th Series, Florence $24.95
2224 World of **Salt Shakers**, 2nd Ed., Lechner $24.95

POTTERY

4312 **Blue & White Stoneware**, McNerney $9.95
1958 So. Potteries **Blue Ridge Dinnerware**, 3rd Ed., Newbound $14.95
1959 **Blue Willow**, 2nd Ed., Gaston $14.95
3816 Collectible **Vernon Kilns**, Nelson $24.95
3311 Collecting **Yellow Ware** – Id. & Value Guide, McAllister $16.95
1373 Collector's Encyclopedia of **American Dinnerware**, Cunningham $24.95
3815 Collector's Encyclopedia of **Blue Ridge Dinnerware**, Newbound $19.95
3272 Collector's Encyclopedia of **California Pottery**, Chipman $24.95
3811 Collector's Encyclopedia of **Colorado Pottery**, Carlton $24.95
2133 Collector's Encyclopedia of **Cookie Jars**, Roerig $24.95
3723 Collector's Encyclopedia of **Cookie Jars**, Volume II, Roerig $24.95
3429 Collector's Encyclopedia of **Cowan Pottery**, Saloff $24.95
2209 Collector's Encyclopedia of **Fiesta**, 7th Ed., Huxford $19.95
3961 Collector's Encyclopedia of **Early Noritake**, Alden $24.95
1439 Collector's Encyclopedia of **Flow Blue China**, Gaston $19.95
3812 Collector's Encyclopedia of **Flow Blue China**, 2nd Ed., Gaston $24.95
3813 Collector's Encyclopedia of **Hall China**, 2nd Ed., Whitmyer $24.95
3431 Collector's Encyclopedia of **Homer Laughlin China**, Jasper $24.95
1276 Collector's Encyclopedia of **Hull Pottery**, Roberts $19.95
4573 Collector's Encyclopedia of **Knowles, Taylor & Knowles**, Gaston $24.95
3962 Collector's Encyclopedia of **Lefton China**, DeLozier $19.95
2210 Collector's Encyclopedia of **Limoges Porcelain**, 2nd Ed., Gaston $24.95
2334 Collector's Encyclopedia of **Majolica Pottery**, Katz-Marks $19.95
1358 Collector's Encyclopedia of **McCoy Pottery**, Huxford $19.95
3963 Collector's Encyclopedia of **Metlox Potteries**, Gibbs Jr. $24.95
3313 Collector's Encyclopedia of **Niloak**, Gifford $19.95
3837 Collector's Encyclopedia of **Nippon Porcelain I**, Van Patten $24.95
2089 Collector's Ency. of **Nippon Porcelain**, 2nd Series, Van Patten $24.95
1665 Collector's Ency. of **Nippon Porcelain**, 3rd Series, Van Patten $24.95
3836 **Nippon Porcelain** Price Guide, Van Patten $9.95
1447 Collector's Encyclopedia of **Noritake**, Van Patten $19.95
3432 Collector's Encyclopedia of **Noritake**, 2nd Series, Van Patten $24.95
1037 Collector's Encyclopedia of **Occupied Japan**, Vol. I, Florence $14.95
1038 Collector's Encyclopedia of **Occupied Japan**, Vol. II, Florence $14.95
2088 Collector's Encyclopedia of **Occupied Japan**, Vol. III, Florence $14.95
2019 Collector's Encyclopedia of **Occupied Japan**, Vol. IV, Florence $14.95
2335 Collector's Encyclopedia of **Occupied Japan**, Vol. V, Florence $14.95
3964 Collector's Encyclopedia of **Pickard China**, Reed $24.95
311 Collector's Encyclopedia of **R.S. Prussia**, 1st Series, Gaston $24.95
715 Collector's Encyclopedia of **R.S. Prussia**, 2nd Series, Gaston $24.95
3726 Collector's Encyclopedia of **R.S. Prussia**, 3rd Series, Gaston $24.95
4877 Collector's Encyclopedia of **R.S. Prussia**, 4th Series, Gaston $24.95
1034 Collector's Encyclopedia of **Roseville Pottery**, Huxford $19.95
1035 Collector's Encyclopedia of **Roseville Pottery**, 2nd Ed., Huxford $19.95
4357 **Roseville** Price Guide No. 10 ....$9.95
1083 Collector's Encyclopedia of **Russel Wright** Designs, Kerr $19.95
3965 Collector's Encyclopedia of **Sascha Brastoff**, Conti, Bethany & Seay $24.95
4314 Collector's Encyclopedia of **Van Briggle** Art Pottery, Sasicki $24.95
2111 Collector's Encyclopedia of **Weller Pottery**, Huxford $29.95
3452 Coll. Guide to Country Stoneware & Pottery, Raycraft $11.95
2077 Coll. Guide to **Country Stoneware & Pottery**, 2nd Series, Raycraft $14.95

3433 Collector's Guide To **Harker Pottery** - U.S.A., Colbert $17.95
3434 Coll. Guide to **Hull Pottery**, The Dinnerware Line, Gick-Burke $16.95
3876 Collector's Guide to **Lu-Ray Pastels**, Meehan $18.95
3814 Collector's Guide to **Made in Japan** Ceramics, White $18.95
4565 Collector's Guide to **Rockingham**, The Enduring Ware, Brewer $14.95
2339 Collector's Guide to **Shawnee Pottery**, Vanderbilt $19.95
1425 **Cookie Jars**, Westfall $9.95
3440 **Cookie Jars**, Book II, Westfall $19.95
3435 Debolt's Dictionary of **American Pottery Marks** $17.95
2379 Lehner's Ency. of **U.S. Marks** on Pottery, Porcelain & China $24.95
3825 **Puritan Pottery**, Morris $24.95
1670 **Red Wing Collectibles**, DePasquale $9.95
1440 **Red Wing Stoneware**, DePasquale $9.95
3738 **Shawnee Pottery**, Mangus $24.95
3327 **Watt Pottery** – Identification & Value Guide, Morris $19.95

OTHER COLLECTIBLES

2269 Antique **Brass & Copper** Collectibles, Gaston $16.95
1880 Antique **Iron**, McNerney $9.95
3872 Antique **Tins**, Dodge $24.95
1714 **Black** Collectibles, Gibbs $19.95
1128 **Bottle** Pricing Guide, 3rd Ed., Cleveland $7.95
3959 **Cereal Box** Bonanza, The 1950's, Bruce $19.95
3718 Collectible **Aluminum**, Grist $16.95
3445 Collectible **Cats**, An Identification & Value Guide, Fyke $18.95
4560 Collectible **Cats**, An Identification & Value Guide, Book II, Fyke $19.95
4563 Collector's Encyclopedia of **Wall Pockets**, Newbound $19.95
1634 Collector's Ency. of Figural & Novelty **Salt & Pepper Shakers**, Davern $19.95
2020 Collector's Ency. of Figural & Novelty **Salt & Pepper Shakers**, Vol. II, Davern ..$19.95
2018 Collector's Encyclopedia of **Granite Ware**, Greguire $24.95
3430 Collector's Encyclopedia of **Granite Ware**, Book II, Greguire $24.95
3879 Collector's Guide to **Antique Radios**, 3rd Ed., Bunis $18.95
1916 Collector's Guide to **Art Deco**, Gaston $14.95
3880 Collector's Guide to **Cigarette Lighters**, Flanagan $17.95
1537 Collector's Guide to **Country Baskets**, Raycraft $9.95
3966 Collector's Guide to **Inkwells**, Identification & Values, Badders $18.95
3881 Collector's Guide to **Novelty Radios**, Bunis/Breed $18.95
3729 Collector's Guide to **Snow Domes**, Guarnaccia $18.95
3730 Collector's Guide to **Transistor Radios**, Bunis $15.95
2276 **Decoys**, Kangas $24.95
1629 **Doorstops**, Identification & Values, Bertoia $9.95
4567 Figural **Napkin Rings**, Gottschalk & Whitson $18.95
3968 **Fishing Lure** Collectibles, Murphy/Edmisten $24.95
3817 **Flea Market Trader**, 10th Ed., Huxford $12.95
3976 Foremost Guide to **Uncle Sam** Collectibles, Czulewicz $24.95
3819 **General Store Collectibles**, Wilson $24.95
2215 Goldstein's **Coca-Cola** Collectibles $16.95
3884 Huxford's Collectible **Advertising**, 2nd Ed. $24.95
2216 **Kitchen Antiques**, 1790–1940, McNerney $14.95
3321 Ornamental & Figural **Nutcrackers**, Rittenhouse $16.95
2026 **Railroad** Collectibles, 4th Ed., Baker $14.95
1632 **Salt & Pepper Shakers**, Guarnaccia $9.95
1888 **Salt & Pepper Shakers** II, Identification & Value Guide, Book II, Guarnaccia ..$14.95
2220 **Salt & Pepper Shakers** III, Guarnaccia $14.95
3443 **Salt & Pepper Shakers** IV, Guarnaccia $18.95
4555 **Schroeder's Antiques Price Guide**, 14th Ed., Huxford $14.95
2096 **Silverplated Flatware**, Revised 4th Edition, Hagan $14.95
1922 Standard **Old Bottle** Price Guide, Sellari $14.95
3892 **Toy & Miniature Sewing Machines**, Thomas $18.95
3828 Value Guide to **Advertising Memorabilia**, Summers $18.95
3977 Value Guide to **Gas Station** Memorabilia, Summers & Priddy $24.95
4572 **Wall Pockets** of the Past, Perkins $17.95
3444 **Wanted to Buy**, 5th Edition $9.95

Schroeder's
ANTIQUES
Price Guide

... is the #1 best-selling antiques & collectibles value guide on the market today, and here's why . . .

Identification & Values Of Over 50,000 Antiques & Collectibles

8½ x 11, 608 Pages, $12.95

• *More than 300 advisors, well-known dealers, and top-notch collectors work together with our editors to bring you accurate information regarding pricing and identification.*

• *More than 45,000 items in almost 500 categories are listed along with hundreds of sharp original photos that illustrate not only the rare and unusual, but the common, popular collectibles as well.*

• *Each large close-up shot shows important details clearly. Every subject is represented with histories and background information, a feature not found in any of our competitors' publications.*

• *Our editors keep abreast of newly developing trends, often adding several new categories a year as the need arises.*

If it merits the interest of today's collector, you'll find it in *Schroeder's*. And you can feel confident that the information we publish is up to date and accurate. Our advisors thoroughly check each category to spot inconsistencies, listings that may not be entirely reflective of market dealings, and lines too vague to be of merit. Only the best of the lot remains for publication.

Without doubt, you'll find
SCHROEDER'S ANTIQUES PRICE GUIDE
the only one to buy for
reliable information and values.

COLLECTOR BOOKS
A Division of Schroeder Publishing Co., Inc.